INSIDE THE MIND (

MICHEL ELTCHANINOFF

Inside the Mind of Marine Le Pen

HURST & COMPANY, LONDON

First published in French by Actes Sud as *Dans la tête de Marine Le Pen* in 2017.
This updated English edition published in the United Kingdom in 2018 by
C. Hurst & Co. (Publishers) Ltd.,
41 Great Russell Street, London, WC1B 3PL

Printed in the United Kingdom by Bell and Bain Ltd, Glasgow

Distributed in the United States, Canada and Latin America by Oxford University Press, 198 Madison Avenue, New York, NY 10016, United States of America.

A Cataloguing-in-Publication data record for this book is available from the British Library.

ISBN: 9781849049344

This book is printed using paper from registered sustainable and managed sources.

www.hurstpublishers.com

CONTENTS

ACKNOWLEDGEMENTS

Thank you to my publisher Michel Parfenov, always magnificent; to Stéphanie Boutonnat and Noël Foiry; to the fine team at *Philosophie Magazine*. Finally, thank you to my friends and to my family, Élisabeth, André, Rébecca and Alexandre, sometimes a little surprised to see me coming back from Front National meetings and to find books with strange titles on my desk.

INTRODUCTION

3 September 2016. A picture-postcard village is hosting the start of Marine Le Pen's electoral campaign. Shortly before midday, several hundred people, cheerful and excited in the late summer sunshine, are waiting for their heroine on the main square at Brachay, a *commune* of some sixty inhabitants in the Haute-Marne department. There are no immigrants here, but people vote for the Front National in large numbers. The setting is perfect, with the stage positioned next to the old town hall with its little bell gable. On the building's side wings one can still make out the inscriptions 'Girls' School' and 'Boys' School'. Behind is a verdant hill, a church and a vast hoarding: 'Marine is saving France'. To the sides of the square marquees have been set up, with tables and plastic chairs inside. Beer and merguez sandwiches are ready for the street party that will follow the speech.

Marine Le Pen makes her entrance onto the platform to chants of 'We're going to win!' and then 'Marine! Marine!' French flags are waved, while a dog barks noisily. The president of the Front National, wearing a dark dress, unhurriedly reads her first major speech as a 2017 presidential election candidate. She pays tribute to Brachay, which in her eyes symbolizes the 'forgotten yet generous and hard-working France', that 'France of the soul and the heart' which 'suffers in silence'. Looking back to the Socialist François Mitterrand's victorious campaign in 1981, Marine Le Pen likewise aspires to embody a 'quiet strength'. Her posters now carry the slogan '*La France apaisée*' ('France at peace'), and the party logo has disappeared. In her almost one-hour speech she takes care to present herself as the candidate of reason; she stresses that she is calling for 'total freedom'. Certain that she will make it to the second round of the election, she is already preparing for the final rally. She spares no effort in consigning her father's Front National to the past, quoting General de Gaulle, *bête noire* of the veterans of French Algeria, and even Montesquieu, the liberal-leaning Enlightenment philosopher.

She depicts herself as the guarantor of republican values and the rule of law. She allows herself to attack Nicolas Sarkozy, a supporter of detention without trial for individuals who appear on the 'S files' and are thus threats to state security. She alone, she proclaims, is capable of applying the rule of law with rigour and firmness. She alone takes into consideration the suffering of those among the French who are impoverished and marginalized. Delivering a lesson in humanism and solidarity, she presses home her message: 'Our project is based on rejecting individualism and the power of money, on refusing to subject mankind to a purely consumerist logic carried out by grasping multinationals.' She denounces Islamist fundamentalism as a 'twenty-first-century totalitarianism', mocks 'antiracism' as 'fundamentally racist', rejects 'mass immigration' (which she likens to 'an absolute tidal wave'), and wishes to abolish 'the aberration of nationality rights'—but she makes sure not to utter a single word that might be considered xenophobic.

She even reminds her audience that the law guarantees the equality of 'all citizens without distinction of origins, race or religion'. The crowd is less enthusiastic about this part of the speech, and one man punctuates Le Pen's declarations with his own, somewhat less politically correct outbursts: 'Queers!'(directed at the US and Germany, to which Paris is apparently subservient); 'Fuck off!' (when she mentions Muslims). Nevertheless, Florian Philippot, a defector from the left whose homosexuality is common knowledge, receives a warm welcome from the crowd, with jovial chanting of 'Florian! Florian!' There are a few aging and tattooed Hell's Angels and a handful of regionalists with the Lorraine flag, but no 'skins' and no '*fachos*' with shaved heads here. Instead people cheerfully show off their T-shirt slogans—'*Je suis Charlie Martel*',[1] 'Arise children of France', 'I'm FN'—with matching Nike shorts and promotional Ricard caps. The young activists are well dressed and look very professional, gathered in conclave like real politicians. They are the movement's future cadres and are eager to hold office. 'Are you going to the pig festival at Hayange tomorrow?' 'No, I've got a meeting at the ecology commission.' As a Johnny Halliday clone performs his recent hits, the atmosphere is somewhere between a gathering at the Tour de France and a professional seminar.

In mid-afternoon buses arrive to take the activists home, all over France. In one of them, heading for Paris, there is plenty of atmosphere and a good deal of discussion. As the vehicle passes Colombey-les-Deux-Églises, a recently recruited supporter suggests that Marine Le Pen's next campaign meeting should take place in General de Gaulle's adopted village: 'A great symbol!' A young man dressed all in black snaps back indignantly: 'De Gaulle? That bastard! He's the one who brought all the Arabs here.' The conversation turns to the media. 'I can't stand them' ... 'all corrupt' ... 'they manipulate people, brainwash them' ... 'the French are like sheep'. Then the anti-Gaullist reveals to his new friends that he 'specializes in Islam'. Tongues are quickly untied: 'Submission, Muslims want submission,' begins one of them. 'Nobody is doing anything about it and they're gradually nibbling away at our country. Soon we'll be in the minority. And France won't be France anymore,' adds another. The self-appointed specialist concludes: 'Islam is essentially intolerant. In any case it's not a religion but an ideology. It's Islamo-Nazism.' General approval.

During a stop at motorway services an old lady is in ecstasy over some red, white and blue lollipops and wants to treat her grandson to one, but he refuses the offer. Several men are looking at a road map of Europe. 'Well, at least they haven't included Turkey!' 'And now they'll have to remove England!' they gloat. The conversation between a woman and two men sitting on the grass is rather more intellectual: 'Good workmanship doesn't exist anymore in France,' says one of the men. 'People just do what they want and as little as possible.' 'Far be it from me to be racist,' says the woman with deliberate irony, 'but it needs to be said: the people on our checkouts are ... exotic to say the least. Maybe this explains why.' She smiles and they all nod in agreement.

Several days later, candidate Le Pen answered a question: is Islam compatible with the Republic? 'Yes, I believe so. An Islam such as the one we have known, secularized by Enlightenment values like other religions.'[2] One can only imagine the disappointment of the anti-Islam militant on the bus back from Brachay. But Marine Le Pen is taking charge. If she wants one day to win a majority of votes she will have to clear the toxic cloud that surrounds the Front National and banish the memory of past xenophobia. The questions we must therefore ask are these: is she offering an ideology compatible with the values of the Republic and stripped of the trappings of far-right thought? Has she turned herself into an ordinary political leader? Or is she carefully polishing her message for purely electoral reasons, while secretly remaining faithful to the fundamentals of *lepéniste* discourse?

One could try to answer such questions with political, semantic or policy analysis. But instead we are going to reread Marine Le Pen's speeches and identify their key ideological elements, including their historical context. From her use of a particular argument or her quotation of a given writer or philosopher, we can discover which movements, schools of thought or authors—perhaps now forgotten—she identifies with.

But first, there is a potential misconception that needs clearing up: Marine Le Pen is not an intellectual. Her father, Jean-Marie, likes to pose as a man of culture, claiming to adore literature and sprinkling his utterances with Latin phrases, obscure words and imperfect subjunctives. His daughter is less pretentious in this regard, and the testimonies of those who have known her contradict any idea of her as a woman of letters.[3] In a tone of voice both charitable and slightly embarrassed, one insider sympathizes that she has so little time to read: 'I can't say that she is steeped in the humanities like her father. It's very different with her ... She finished high school and then studied law. But because of her job she spends her time reading political works, notes or technical files. It's very time-consuming!' The implication is clear: Marine Le Pen never cracks the spine of a book. Another source, who says he admires the father's extensive appreciation of culture, is more dubious about the daughter: 'I ask myself what her father handed down to her. There's a break rather than continuity.' More cruelly, a final witness recounts how one day he referred to the march on Rome that allowed Mussolini to take power in 1922. Marine Le Pen, according to him, had never heard of it. At least, he smiles, it proves that she's not inherited much from fascism!

In her defence, Le Pen's childhood was hardly conducive to the calm needed for the handing down of culture. She saw very little of her parents, who never took her on holiday. She was brought up in the company of a nanny, on a separate floor from her parents' rooms. In 1976, when she was eight years old, the family apartment in Paris' fifteenth arrondissement was blown up in a deliberate attack.[4] She was then nearly smothered by a psychopath.[5] Installed with her two elder sisters, Marie-Caroline and Yann, at Montretout, a sumptuous property in Saint-Cloud, she endured her parents' sudden and bitter divorce. 'I would have liked it if my parents ... had shown a little more interest and paid more attention to me, including my education, because there as well I was left to struggle on my own,' she laments in her autobiography.[6] What her father, who was often absent, bequeathed to her, she says, was not an intellectual inheritance so much as an 'ethical, moral education'.[7]

Out in the real world, she had to bear the cross of being Jean-Marie Le Pen's daughter when faced with teachers she describes as malicious.[8] During her law studies she acquired a reputation as a 'clubber', yet also as someone who made waves, surrounded by members of the GUD, the extreme-right student organization, at its alma mater, the Assas faculty in Paris.[9] She seemed to prefer French pop music to the literary classics. She became a criminal defence lawyer but found it hard to attract clients, again because of her name. She quickly began to hold positions of responsibility within the party. She married, had three children, divorced, remarried, and divorced again. It was only when she rose through the ranks of the Front National, according to a close friend, that 'she worked on index cards to develop her knowledge of political and historical culture'.[10]

A more recent episode seems to confirm such off-the-record anecdotes. At the end of the 2000s, the former MEP Paul-Marie Coûteaux became close to Marine Le Pen. A left-wing Gaullist and sovereigntist allied to cross-spectrum political heavyweights such as Jean-Pierre Chevènement, Philippe Séguin, Charles Pasqua and Nicolas Dupont-Aignan, he founded a small political party, SIEL (Sovereignty, Independence and Liberties), which supported the Front National. In late 2011 he became one of Marine Le Pen's spokesmen. This intellectual has published several books in which he defends the 'genius of Christianity' and the classical tradition—the two components, according to him, of French identity. In September 2010 Coûteaux undertook Le Pen's political education, drawing up a reading list.[11] In the history book category, he recommended *Histoire de France* (1924) by Jacques Bainville, a monarchist historian close to Charles Maurras and his far-right, counter-revolutionary Action française movement:

> Its 580 pages are themselves worth several years spent studying political science: not only do they restore the entire history of France from the Gauls up to Clemenceau (the history ends there) but above all these pages, very easy to read, reveal the constants in France's politics, a permanent politics from century to century—until it was pulverized thirty years ago.

Coûteaux advised Le Pen to be cautious, however. It would be better to quote Tocqueville, the liberal nineteenth-century historian, than Gaxotte, who positioned himself on the far right in the interwar years:

> I shall leave to one side the excellent Gaxotte, whom you know, I think, and I believe he should not be quoted too often; just as authors who are too far to the right shouldn't be quoted, as it gives the impression of waffling: it's better to refer to authors of the left or those who are universally recognized as classic, among whom many say what we are saying. Mentioning them gives weight to our words.

The reading list included philosophers such as Plato who supported the notion of a social hierarchy, counter-revolutionary authors such as Chateaubriand, but also 'writers more to the left, of the insurgent type, like Vallès and Zola'. 'These are authors who also suit you,' suggested Coûteaux, encouraging Le Pen to read Zola's 'very working-class *Germinal*, a terrific epic set in the northern coal mines; or *Au Bonheur des Dames*, the trials and tribulations of small business.' The 'professor' had firmly grasped the importance of social themes in the discourse of his student, the future president of the FN. Finally, among contemporaries, Coûteaux singled out the anti-modernist essayist Philippe Muray: 'It all opens the mind and renews our political ground: with Muray's words you will find countless allies with whom to mock the *bobo* [bougie], capitalist and consumerist world.' He also urged Le Pen to read Michel Houellebecq's novel *Atomised* (*Les Particules élémentaires*), 'a description of the seediest side of modernity, the insipidness of easy pleasure, the death of desire, relativism, greyness, general vulgarity', and the *Journal* of Renaud Camus, 'an author disliked by the right-minded' for his denunciations of 'immigrationist madness, the collapse of schooling, the eradication of civilization'—in short, as Coûteaux put it, 'the essence of our concerns'.

When reminded of this politico-pedagogical episode, Coûteaux, now on less friendly terms with the FN leader, smiles: 'Marine never mentioned it to me again; yet I'd tried to act as a teacher. Even though she herself had asked me to help her address her lack of education, I wonder whether she objected to the note I sent her with this in mind. Was it too complex? Maybe she thought I was making fun of her...'[12] And yet one finds dotted around in Le Pen's speeches allusions to several of the authors on the list.

Her supposed lack of education makes an investigation into the 'Marinist' Front National's ideology a risky undertaking. Again according to Paul-Marie Coûteaux, 'there is hardly any ideology in the FN. Ideas end up in a sort of "junk room" that nobody tries to clear up. Florian Philippot, whom I introduced to Marine Le Pen in 2009, is a pure "statocrat"—I had thought that he would be able to give her a little culture of government, to instil some order in her cabinet, but I hadn't imagined that he would become her main, and even only, adviser. His only strength is the state; the state is everything for him.'

> He's hardly interested in the nation, by which I mean the nation in terms of our History, which he doesn't know very well, nor in terms of geography, which he doesn't seem to know any better; nor is he greatly interested in the singularity of French civilization and in particular its profound Christian heritage. Education, the University, the French language, cultural policy, protecting landscapes and the environment in general—as a good economist (or rather a good modernist who reduces political concerns to economic concerns), he is not inspired by any of this. He hasn't felt any more concerned by the debate over what is (mis)named 'marriage for all' [gay marriage]. He's neither for nor against: it doesn't interest him. If you talk to him about

> 'natural law', even though it nourishes all of France's 'being in the world', he just looks blank.
>
> Essentially he believes in a sovereignty without substance. Sovereignty, for him, can be reduced to legal and economic questions. For me, that's secondary. For me as a Gaullist (he says he's a Gaullist too, but I think he's only familiar with a simplified, nursery school version of de Gaulle), the vital thing is the sovereignty of nation and civilization, but he doesn't see what it's all about.[13]

Jean-Claude Martinez, a former senior leader of the Front National, puts forward another argument: 'Marine Le Pen doesn't have any ideas. She only acts through instinct, because her brain is like a reptile's. What ideas? What concepts? She's an echo chamber, that's all!'[14] According to an expert on the far right, Jean-Yves Camus, 'the FN is in an advanced process of de-ideologization', in which it has become a power-winning machine driven by simple themes. As such, 'the development of ideology takes place outside the party. The Front National publishes very little and doesn't even have a newspaper. *National Hebdo* has ceased to exist; *Rivarol* takes [Le Pen Senior]'s line; *Présent*, the voice of the Catholic traditionalists, is a shadow of its former self.' The strength of the FN is in 'gathering a significant section of the electorate around a political project, at the heart of which ideology plays a less and less important part.' Indeed, he continues,

> this political family has suffered since 1945 from a stigma that it carries like a convict's iron chains. Many express the view that at the Liberation fascism and Nazism discredited every sort of nationalism. For these parties to become acceptable as coalition partners or in power, they always have to show more proof of having broken with a past that many don't want them to leave behind.[15]

As a result, they'll do everything they can to wipe away all trace of the far right.

A clumsy cobbling together of contradictory tendencies, the absence of original thought, the abandonment of ideology—these are some of the obstacles to examining the ideas put forward by Marine Le Pen. It is true that her speeches sometimes resemble heavy patchworks, edited and corrected by so many hands that they end up indigestible, barely coherent and repetitious.[16] Yet surely the extent of the FN's popular support must be explained by some comprehensive view of the world? The ideology of Marine Le Pen's FN, even if it is an amalgam, does in fact exist. Not only does it possess a certain coherence, but it is also linked to movements, past and present, with a real intellectual basis. But before analysing the discourse of the new Front National, we must first understand the ideological foundations of the old.

1

THE FOUR PILLARS OF THE FAR RIGHT

It is the mid-1980s, rue de Rivoli in Paris, and the French far right is commemorating Joan of Arc.[1] Catholic traditionalists are brandishing images of the Sacred Heart of Jesus as they pray aloud in Latin. A cohort of revolutionary nationalists goose-steps past, while Pétainists, in their tweed and pleated skirts, display their portraits of the marshall. The skinheads, Doc Martens on their feet, like to show off their tattoos and bomber jackets; the royalists of Action française prefer more formal attire and a very 'inter-war' walking stick. Then there are the intellectuals in their crumpled raincoats, and those who still yearn for a lost French Algeria.

Since the Second World War, the French far right has been made up a mosaic of small groups with sometimes antagonistic ideological differences. It took the political talent of one Jean-Marie Le Pen to force them to co-exist, with the forming of his party in 1972. As Jean-Yves Camus puts it,

> Jean-Marie Le Pen brought this political family out of the ghetto where it had been segregated since the war. And he brought together, in a rickety coalition, collaborators and resistance fighters, former communists and anti-communists, liberals and statists, Gaullists and anti-Gaullists, traditionalist Catholics and neo-pagans, conservatives and revolutionary nationalists, royalists and democrats.[2]

Bruno Gollnisch, formerly number two in the Front National, explains the secret of Le Pen's success: 'When you're in the trenches facing the enemy, you don't ask the man next to you whether he goes to Mass.'[3] Differences must be downplayed in the name of a struggle against a common enemy. This is the 'nationalist compromise', theorized by Charles Maurras, founder of the monarchist Action française, during the First World War.

But does the fact that Jean-Marie Le Pen managed to unite all the factions of the French far right enable us to define his ideology? How, indeed, can this be done given that it is made up of so many currents? Besides, the far right spurns the idea of submitting itself to a unified, rational political line. According to Jean-Yves Camus,

> it is the prerogative of the right to have a world view that is not as mechanistic, structured and globalizing as that of the left. The right is based on a certain number of attitudes. It is more attuned to style than to ideology. The 'driving images' underpinning its outlook are fleeting lightning flashes that determine its pivotal ideas.

> There is nothing more alien to the right-wing mentality than the idea of sticking to a system.[4]

And yet it is possible to sketch a synthetic description of far-right thinking. This general philosophy is not homogenous and sometimes takes contradictory political forms, but it follows an overall logic and common founding principles. In short, this body of thought stands in opposition to the eighteenth-century Enlightenment movement, which wanted to replace submission to authority, religious belief and obedience to tradition with independence of the individual, rationalism and freedom. The questioning of such Enlightenment values began with the Romantic period, and from the end of the eighteenth century in Germany and the start of the nineteenth in France, there was a growing tendency to glorify the past and Christianity as well as to extol national languages, the fantastic and folklore tradition. At the end of the nineteenth century, writers and philosophers intensified this reaction, in opposition to the consequences of the Enlightenment, which they identified as representative democracy, individualism, bourgeois prosperity, atheism, the rule of law, belief in progress through science, universalism and humanism.

As such, far-right thought revolves around four principal themes: the land, the people, life and myth. Each of these (and sometimes several at the same time) can be attributed to the forefathers or other members of this anti-Enlightenment bloodline. Some caution is required here: a thinker who may have embraced one such theme cannot automatically be classed as far-right. Yet he or she may, even inadvertently, have served as a source of inspiration for that political current. What unites most theorists within this school of thought is a particular way of interpreting and articulating these four themes.

The notion of land or soil is an obsession of the far right. During the Enlightenment century, thinkers dreamed of cosmopolitanism and 'the right of common possession of the surface of the earth'.[5] Over ancient regions, the French Revolution superimposed the abstract administrative entities that are the *départements*. Politics became a matter of universal ideals, law and rationality. In reaction, towards the end of the nineteenth century some writers promoted the notion of the soil, an idea that expressed a primordial attachment to the world. Political life, they proposed, should not consist of abstract ideals but of feeling a remembered and visceral familiarity with a *terroir* (soil, land, often local). The notion was that being rooted in a landscape and a region determined a specific way of looking at the world.

The wisdom drawn from the soil brought with it a condemnation of *déracinés*, the deracinated or rootless, contaminated by universalist ideology: democrats or freemasons, but also foreigners and Jews. In Germany, Carl Schmitt (1888–1985), one of the official jurists and theorists of the Nazi regime, turned soil (*Boden*) into the principle behind a combat between civilizations: 'world history is the history of the struggle of maritime powers against continental powers'.[6] In his *Land und Meer* (1942), he argued for a 'politics of earth': 'Man is a terrestrial, an earthling. He lives, moves and walks on the firmly-grounded Earth. It is his standpoint and his base. He derives his points of view from it, which is also to say that his impressions are determined by it and his world outlook is conditioned by it.'[7] The sea, conversely, is symbolic of a lack of limits and restraint, for the ocean is not bound by any frontiers. It is no coincidence that, in his eyes, the sea is the fundamental element of the Atlanticist Anglo-Saxons—and the Jews. It was also at this time that 'Blood, soil, honour and loyalty' became a Nazi motto.

The theme of the people constitutes the second pillar of the far right's thinking, but here it must be understood in a very different sense from that expounded by Jean-Jacques Rousseau or Jean Jaurès, who used the concept within a framework of democracy, nationhood, progress and ties of fraternity and solidarity. On the contrary, far-right theorists see the notion in terms of identity, and as such 'the people' does not signify the sum total of all citizens. In the nineteenth century, pseudo-scientific racialist thought sought to split humankind into a hierarchy of different peoples. In his *Essai sur l'inégalité des races humaines* (Essay on the Inequality of the Human Races,1853–5), Arthur de Gobineau (1816–82) distinguished between black, yellow and white races, affirmed the superiority of the latter and proposed that a people enters a state of degeneration when it 'no longer has in its veins the same blood, the value of which has been damaged by continual miscegenation'.

With mixed blood seen as a cause of decadence, the notion of race exploded the traditional meaning given to 'the people', transcending nationhood and promising hitherto unknown territorial reconfigurations. Besides the foreigner, the Jew became the ideal scapegoat, with the idea of a people polluted by the enemy within forming the basis of Nazi thought. Another, social, interpretation of the people places it in opposition to 'the elite(s)'. Several models of a proto-fascist National Socialism were elaborated from the end of the nineteenth century up to the Second World War, in which, in the name of a collective whole, the selfish individualism of the Enlightenment came under fire. In contrast to the so-called cosmopolitan (in other words, Jewish) elites stood the values of the common people: rootedness in a particular place, restraint, solidarity and conservatism.

With the concept of life, the far right's ideologues contrast the laws of nature and the physicality of the body with the growing abstraction of the modern world. The Italian Futurists fostered ideas of youth, speed, energy and the power of the will,[8] and fascism added to this an apologia of war as a purifying process, the apotheosis of life through its confrontation with death. In an ethical and aesthetic conception of courage, martial comradeship and heroism, the soldier, often a volunteer escaping the boredom of bourgeois life, comes face to face with his true self. Militarism, with its discipline, uniforms, decorations, virile parades and phalanxes, enhances this vision of the world.

A further manifestation of this bellicose mentality is the anticipated and hoped-for *coup* that will overthrow rotten institutions. In the logic of the revolutionary far right, the call to insurrection is considered a dynamic and vital movement within the order of things. Representative democracy and the stable rule of law are hence viewed as deadly abstractions, and to this is attached the cult of the leader. Hierarchy is intrinsic to the natural world, as in the thought of Plato, or Hinduism's caste structure, and this is how the fascist understanding of the state should be read. Far from an abstract institution representing the sum of individual aspirations, it stands as the culmination of human existence, and in return, the state shapes all of society within its totalitarian project, forming a vast body of which it is the head. And if society is perceived as an organism, it is also analysed in medical terms; it is either healthy or diseased, or contaminated by foreign bodies. The language of physical reflex and instinct is all-important.

The final pillar is that of myth. Since the Protestant Reformation, a critical reading of the founding texts of our religious culture has prevailed, and a scientific approach first to nature and then to history emerged.

Thus myth substitutes this rational discourse with another language that is simultaneously contemporary and deliberately archaic. A pessimistic vision of history gathered force at the beginning of the twentieth century and gave birth to the myth of decline. Obsessed by the notion of decadence, certain writers ceased believing in the progress of human knowledge, turning instead to a cyclical conception of evolution. Oswald Spengler (1880–1936), author of *The Decline of the West*, an immense success throughout Europe, inspired all those who, at the end of the

Great War, believed in the end of one world—and sometimes in a redefinition of civilization. The idea of a purifying catastrophe haunted some minds, while disillusionment with scientific and technological modernity pushed many thinkers towards tradition—in other words elements of ancient culture, both magical and religious, whether Persian, Indian or Celtic, but since rejected by the rational mind.[9] Rebellion against democratic institutions and the ideas of human rights and progress was advocated under the aegis of paganism.[10] The sickly sweet Christianity of pity and evangelism (considered to be of Semitic origin) was to be replaced with the glorification of the cruel divinities of the ancient or oriental worlds.

Such immersion in myth went hand in hand with a fascination with secret societies, and some myth makers, sometimes members of occult groups (the Thule Society in Germany, for instance), were obsessed by conspiracies, especially those involving the Other: the Jewish plot supposedly contained in *The Protocols of the Elders of Zion*[11] or masonic domination. A taste for myths ultimately gave birth to the phantasm, shared by Soviet ideologues, of a New Man. The thinkers of Italian fascism called for the transcendence of ordinary humanity by a being rendered invincible, a man who required a grandiose setting: Mussolinian or Nazi architecture or spectacular rallies. The aesthetic dimension of fascism thrived in this renaissance of mythology, also to be found in the pompous neoclassical style of Stalinism.

To reiterate, these themes, if taken in isolation, are not always enough to identify far-right thinking. But when put together, and when they all fit under the banner of hatred for the rule of law and progress, they form a very recognizable whole. So were these the four pillars holding up the old Front National led by Jean-Marie Le Pen?

2

DADDY'S FN

12 July 2016, Saint-Cloud, in the Parisian suburbs. Right at the back of the private park of Montretout, which shelters billionaires' residences, is the entrance to the Le Pen family home. Marine used to live in a converted loft in the old servants' quarters. She left towards the end of 2014, several months before her official break with her father. The reason for this departure? A Doberman belonging to the patriarch appears—symbolically—to have killed one of his daughter's cats... One of the dogs growls, unreassuringly, at the arrival of a visitor. The man who opens the garden gate is unsmiling when asked whether the Molossus bites or eats people alive: 'It depends who,' he replies with icy indifference. Then there's a wait on the ground floor of the main building, in a somewhat rundown Second Empire sitting room.

Jean-Marie Le Pen is upstairs in his first-floor office, with its panoramic view over Paris. The style is bourgeois, but not flashy—in its original state. The room is crowded with objects: knickknacks and books, portraits and photos of the FN's historic leader, statuettes and model ships. Le Pen, eighty-four years old, is wearing an immaculate midnight blue suit and a shirt with no tie. As I sit down opposite him, he seems surly and uncommunicative. On his desk sits an enormous calendar decorated with the effigy of Vladimir Putin. The former president of the FN has agreed to outline his cultural and philosophical tastes, his party's ideology and his own view of the world. My task is to discover whether such tastes and views correspond to the four pillars of the extreme right.

First and foremost, which philosophers have inspired Le Pen? 'I don't feel I'm a philosopher,' he concedes. 'I'm more of a man of action. But I have read a great many works of philosophy.' Which? 'I would feel I was betraying the truth saying anything that was inaccurate. I don't sense that I belong to any one school of philosophy more than another.' At the suggestion of Nietzsche and his life apologia, he replies, 'I don't feel a great affinity with the German philosophers. I recognize the value and strength of a certain number of their propositions, but I don't feel comfortable with either their thinking or their expression. It's instinctive.' He then moves immediately onto his musical tastes. 'On the other hand, there are certain pieces of music that are models for me, like Beethoven's 'Violin Concerto in D major'. He suddenly brightens up and starts humming, to a military march rhythm: 'Tin, tin tin tin, tin tin, tin tin tin, tin tin...' He now seems more at ease, and continues: 'I know songs by the hundred. I have a repertoire that ranges from the religious to the erotic, from the guard room, the Foreign Legion's military marches, royalist or anarchist songs to the songs of Tino Rossi!' He then turns seamlessly to poetry and starts reciting emphatically, hardly pausing for breath:

J'ai perdu ma force et ma vie,
Et mes amis et ma gaieté;
J'ai perdu jusqu'à la fierté
Qui faisait croire à mon génie.

Quand j'ai connu la Vérité,
J'ai cru que c'était une amie;
Quand je l'ai comprise et sentie,
J'en étais déjà dégoûté.[1]

'Musset,' he concludes, in a tragic tone of voice. When pressed to name his favourite authors, he evades the question: 'I've read so much that I can't recall what's had an influence on me. It's poets more than philosophers who have influenced me.' But which ones, now? He consents to mention one name: 'One of them most particularly: Robert Brasillach [1909–45]. He is one of the few poets to have been condemned to death, like André Chénier during the French Revolution. Brasillach wrote his *Poèmes de Fresnes* before he died, aged thirty-five.' So the only author cited by Jean-Marie Le Pen as one of his inspirations is a figure of the French far right, formerly of the monarchist Action française and then editor of the collaborationist and anti-Semitic newspaper *Je suis partout*. Then, as if to soften his choice, he also lists La Fontaine, Corneille, Racine and Supervielle.

When asked about the ideological tenets of the party he led for decades, he sticks to a minimalist definition:

> A national, popular and social right. It was first about opposing a left that, at that time, was communist, socialist, radical and masonic. That also drove away the moderate right. After the Liberation the country moved in the opposite direction from the French state's formula, which in any case predated Pétain: 'Work, family, fatherland.' Post-war politics was built on the antithesis of those values that were reputedly fascist or in any case nefarious. But our current was very attached to the values of the fatherland, implying a values structure that is particularly concerned with the family. Patriotism is attachment to the soil, to one's origins, to history, to identity, to the historic projection of the national community, first and foremost French-speaking, of course.

Besides the political definition of the FN, on what deep foundations does its ideology rest? Jean-Marie Le Pen now sets out his worldview. The starting point for *lepéniste* philosophy is the idea of decline: 'Our civilization is in a state of decadence. This can largely be attributed to the collapse of religious values in our society since the 1960s and the Second Vatican Council' (1962–5), whose aim was to adapt the Catholic Church to the contemporary world. 'Before that,' he continues,

> French society had been profoundly shaped by Christian religion. All of human existence was framed by it, from the first steps of baptism up to death and the funeral service. The abandonment of what I believe to be essential, ritual—gestures, words, chanting, with their aesthetic notations, ornamental, musical and symbolic—has led to a very real break. As for the expectation of resurrection, it offered an optimistic answer to the question of eternity and the dark void into which we fall when we cease breathing. That fed into an emotional dimension of life, but it has suddenly collapsed.

What caused the collapse of religious practice? A 'demographic depression, which brought about the ruin of spiritual, moral, mental and psychological structures.' And what, in turn, brought about that depression?

> The professional promotion of women outside the family, sexual egalitarianism. Although men and women are profoundly different, and although nature has programmed women to assure the reproduction of the species as their essential task, the feminization of society has encouraged women's independence and turned them away from the vital function of reproduction. Women have taken the place of men during periods of great conflict, in 1914–18 or 1939–45. Women have made advances through necessity, have got used to it

> and enjoy it. Those who have studied feel the urge to have a child at around thirty-five, which is too late to ensure generational renewal.

All of the post-war era, then, is to be rejected in the name of a past which—it can hardly be a coincidence—corresponds to the childhood of Jean-Marie Le Pen. This backward-looking yearning surrounds the far right's recurring motifs: the myth of decline, the way the people have lost identity, demographic slowdown, the disappearance of roots, antipathy towards foreigners and freemasons, nostalgia for the anti-republican Pétainist state, anti-egalitarianism, rejection of individual autonomy and criticism of society's 'feminization'.

The success of the Front National from the 1980s was built on hostility towards immigrants. In a pseudo-scientific schema, Le Pen now elaborates his basic message (immigration = insecurity + unemployment) into a broader exposition. According to him,

> mass immigration follows on from the demographic revolution. One only had to identify the probable consequences in the decadent world we know to understand what would happen in due course. The strength of the Front National is that it concentrated its activity from the outset on issues that would become topical years later.

He gives more examples, providing statistics. 'In Africa, the demographic explosion is of uncontrollable proportions. In fifty years there will be 440 million inhabitants in Nigeria. There are upheavals there which are physical, social, spiritual, and religious, which are innately revolutionary and are going to submerge a civilization like ours...' Le Pen then recycles the myth of the soil, using the term 'boreal Europe', one of the favourite concepts of certain far-right currents during the 1960s.

> Boreal Europe, which stretches from Brest to Vladivostok, shares the vast geostrategic area of Siberia. Now, it has little time in which to ensure its survival. If this doesn't materialize with dynamic initiatives in geographical terms and protective steps in security terms, it will be submerged by covert forms of invasion, since these will not be military.

Such invasions, says Le Pen, come from the south but also from the east, in the form of the Chinese who live and work in Siberia. He confides that he will soon be going to Russia to offer his help in the struggle against the new yellow peril.

Opposition to immigration from outside Europe is based on a conviction of cultural inequality, as this aside testifies. Referring to pre-war pedagogy, which consisted of 'taking advantage of the exceptional accessibility of the young mind in order to fill heads with the cultural material they could draw on later,' he continues: 'There comes a time when one loses that ability to absorb. As a supporter of French Algeria and of the integration of the Muslim populations, I had studied the question of education. I had noticed that Europeans' intellectual progression forges ahead in a straight line, drops off slightly at thirteen, then continues in an upwards trajectory. In the Muslim world, at eleven or twelve, bam! Everything suddenly stops.' Why? Le Pen moves his raised hand in a suggestive gesture and whispers: 'Masturbation. As Europeans, we are not prone to this sexual obsession because of our religion, which controls such impulses, as far as it can. The success of our civilization is due to the conscious holding back of sexuality, whereas among simple people it is let loose. With religious peoples like ours, it is resisted and mastered, creating a dynamism, an economy of means, time and mobilization.' Suddenly excited and articulate, the veteran of French Algeria delves into his memories with ribald jokes, recalling an eminent university professor in Algiers, who, behind his lofty, high-brow appearance, 'was just thinking about a black woman's big arse'.

This interlude, which seems to transport Le Pen back to a blessed moment in his existence, in Algeria, doesn't prevent him from expressing the essentials of his worldview. Faced with the decadence and invasion that threaten to damage the superiority of our civilization, 'the FN wants to stress that societies have basic rules, and those that don't respect [our] elementary norms are destined to disappear.' He lays out his credo:

> My philosophy is one of survivalism, because life is a fight, a permanent contest against adversity, depending more or less on luck. It may be more pleasant to stay

> sitting in an armchair than to march under a hot sun, but the only way you can be sure of keeping your independence is not to stay in the armchair. Essentially, I can express my philosophy of action in the words of a parachute regiment's motto: "*Être et durer*."[2] We don't have much time. Humankind itself could completely disappear, particularly after a nuclear war. Anyway, I try to convince my compatriots that they should give themselves a month of survival with a sack of rice, some tinned food and some water, as it's probable that food supplies will one day run out. In the event of a real crisis, supermarkets won't last twenty-four hours, they'll be looted and burnt down. Imagine if the water system was attacked and stopped working. Only those who had put some bottled water to one side would survive. Though water isn't really completely indispensable ... if you've got some wine.

He laughs again.

His final remarks are even more disconcerting. First he poses as the misunderstood prophet. 'I have my doubts about saying all that since I'm going to be accused of apocalypticism. Lucidity carries its own risks. A good turn is never forgiven.' Then he addresses the difference of opinion that has set him against his daughter Marine. 'I led a movement for forty years and then I found myself—an extraordinary state of affairs in politics—excluded from my own party by my daughter who is my successor,[3] at precisely the moment that the planned growth in strength was happening, as I had envisaged it. It was at the moment that I was proven right that they thought things would happen quicker without me. It was a sin of pride. The individuals who are now at the head of the movement take the credit for its electoral successes, when really those successes are the culmination of a long march and the coming together of events predicted long ago.' After this clarification, Jean-Marie Le Pen indulges in a little mock despair. 'Gone with the wind. When I die, it will be an entire library going up in flames. Everything that I've learnt will count for nothing. *Sic transit gloria mundi*...' Then he alludes to the difficulties of translating into and from Latin: 'Watch out for the enemy. The devil is in the detail ... as Le Pen would say...'

The interview is over. Provocation has merged with theory, childhood memories and jokes in questionable taste. Better not to dwell on the man's psychology, which reveals a certain infantilism—his ideal world strangely resembling that of his early years—as well as a mix of meandering theory and buffoonery. But as far as his ideas are concerned, all the ingredients of the far-right corpus are present. The guiding principle of existence is a battling life force. That of history is the myth of decay and decline. The basis of politics is the vision of a European people defending its soil against the invader.

Now, the question is what, if anything, of these ideological roots can be found in the thought of his daughter.

3

THE HUMAN FACE OF NATIONALISM

Jean-Marie Le Pen likes playing the role of the villain. Conscious that his party was once a small sect, he turned its media misdemeanours into a strategy: 'It doesn't matter whether they say good or bad things about us. The main thing is that they talk about us,' he declared in *Rivarol*.[1] At Montretout he affirmed that 'the FN's strength lies in its otherness. It's not like the others.'[2] The election of Donald Trump in the United States comforted him in this conviction. In this context, it is easy for Marine Le Pen to highlight the shift in direction that she seems to have imposed on the party by normalizing it or, to use the term current within the FN itself, by de-demonizing, or detoxifying, it.[3]

Yet the theory that the FN has undergone a recent and definitive change is not entirely accurate. In reality, the party's history is intertwined with a series of such detoxifications. Even its creation in 1972 was a response to the desire to give a respectable face to the anti-

Semitic, violent and neo-fascist far right of the period. The group Ordre nouveau (New Order) asked Jean-Marie Le Pen, a former parliamentary deputy and well-known politician, to act as its 'shop window' in the hope of winning votes and seats.[4] Le Pen was also in a position to unite a diverse range of individuals and political tendencies around his relative notoriety. According to Louis Aliot (MEP, vice-president of the party—and incidentally Marine Le Pen's partner), while Le Pen Senior brought together 'patriots' of differing sorts, he sought above all and from the start to extricate the FN from the traditions of the far right. He wanted, says Aliot

> to get people who had historically been enemies around the same table. He thought it was time to stop rubbing salt into wounds and instead to talk about the future. That's how those who were Gaullists in 1940 and anti-Gaullists in 1960 found themselves in the FN. Le Pen stood the test of time because his private address book went far beyond the fringes of the traditional far right. He was a former parachutist in the Foreign Legion and had been a deputy during the Fourth Republic [1946–58]. Moreover, the hardliners in the OAS had it in for Le Pen for not supporting them.[5]

Le Pen thus appeared as a conciliator, a much more reassuring figure than his militant rank-and-file. In the 1980s, when the FN was experiencing its first electoral successes, a second phase of detoxification took place. The leaders of the movement known as the Nouvelle

Droite (New Right)—which aimed not to win elections, but to implant far-right ideas into society and the media and to change general attitudes—formulated neologisms aimed at making the FN's rhetoric more respectable. Bruno Mégret and Jean-Yves Le Gallou created the concept of 'national preference', considered to be more positive and closer to an unthreatening sort of common sense than the xenophobic slogan of expelling foreigners.

However, the euphemistic nature of the new terms employed and the professionalization of the party's political communication could barely contend with Jean-Marie's penchant for anti-Semitic provocation: the list of 'lying' and 'persecuting' journalists, all with names of Jewish origin: 'Jean-François Kahn, Jean Daniel, Ivan Levaï, Elkabbach' (October 1985); gas chambers judged to be a 'detail of the history of the Second World War' (13 September 1987); the pun on the name of the then civil service minister 'Durafour-crématoire' (September 1988);[6] the notion that 'the German occupation had not been particularly inhumane' (January 2005); the *fournée* (oven load) promised to the Jewish singer Patrick Bruel and other artists (June 2014), and so on. The fact remains that such remarks are insidiously pitched as asides or jokes, serving only to underline their vileness, but also allowing Le Pen to claim that his motives are impugned at the same time as conniving with those who understand all too well.

Marine Le Pen, for her part, puts centre stage a discourse of breaking with the past, wanting to turn the FN into a party like any other, fully integrated into the republican game. Whereas her father believes that the FN is attractive because it is transgressive, she thinks that the party will never come to power while it is suspected of being racist and anti-republican. She has therefore inserted a whole series of corrections into the FN's traditional discourse. Belonging to a different generation from that of its historic leaders, she claims to be unfamiliar with the classic culture of the far right. She even alleges that she has been reproached 'for not knowing the words to "Maréchal nous voilà"[7] or for not reciting Maurras or Léon Bloy verbatim.'[8]

With his open expression and blue eyes, Nicolas Bay looks the part—something of the ideal *frontiste* son-in-law. Born into a middle-class Catholic family, he began to campaign, aged fourteen, against the Maastricht Treaty after attending one of Jean-Marie Le Pen's meetings. Having left the party for a while with Bruno Mégret, who spilt from the FN, Bay has returned to the heart of 'the firm', where he is 'doing quite well'. Today he has an electoral fiefdom in Normandy at his command; he is an MEP and, since 2014, secretary-general of the party. This admirer of the Napoleonic myth is an expert in matters of strategy and systems. He sums up what distinguishes the leadership of the FN's founder from that of his daughter:

> Jean-Marie Le Pen made the various cliques, which were each acting with a feudal mentality, co-exist. The party was divided into clans: traditionalist Catholics, neo-pagans, etc. With Marine, it's the opposite. She believes that everyone can have their own personal convictions but that everybody must follow the movement's line. The slightest difference of opinion will be used by our opponents to underline supposed schisms. She demands, in the context of the professionalization of the Front, that each person's personal, philosophical or religious convictions remain in the private domain and that all should take care to defend the party line alone. This forces discipline onto a political family that has always been structurally undisciplined. This is all the more essential as the 'neither right nor left' strategy brings us people from other horizons than the usual electorate of the national right.[9]

In short, in the new FN, one can think what one likes, but one can only say what has been approved by the party, and it is very noticeable that statements made by leaders such as Louis Aliot, Wallerand de Saint-Just or Nicolas Bay are extremely controlled and are meant to seem consensual. Marine Le Pen, on the other hand, must galvanize her audiences when making speeches, and she, as we will see, can appear much more virulent.

Since 2011, Marine Le Pen has encouraged several significant changes within FN ideology. Firstly, and most spectacularly, she has renounced her father's latent anti-Semitism. Scarcely a few days after her accession to the presidency of the party, she made herself extremely clear with remarks that sounded like a direct riposte to her father and which sought to remove any ambiguity: 'Everybody knows what happened in the concentration camps and under what conditions. What happened was the epitome of barbarity. And believe me, I shall not forget it.'[10] Faced with the indignation caused by her father's remarks about Patrick Bruel and the *fournée*, she insisted that 'the Front National condemns in the strongest terms all forms of anti-Semitism, however expressed.'[11] The desire to give the FN a non-anti-Semitic face is obvious. Louis Aliot, who comes from a family faithful to French Algeria, joined the party in 1988 and was for a long time close to Jean-Marie Le Pen, whom he defends in every respect—apart from his anti-Semitic indiscretions.

> He's hard to understand sometimes. The 'detail of history' business will always be a great mystery to me. It was an outrageous remark that was utterly pointless. Having discussed it with him dozens of times, I know he doesn't believe it, but he thinks that provocation is the only way to make a political project move forwards. And yet for the 2 per cent of those on the far right whom he attracts, how many more does he scare? In fact, anti-Semitism shocks non-Jews the most, and that is obvious in electoral campaigns. The only thing that comes up is the 'detail' [of history] question. People say to us: "Le Pen's OK, but then again, the 'detail'." Marine

> is very much aware of it. De-demonization is about this and this alone.[12]

More generally, Marine Le Pen is leaving behind the racist image attached to her party. We should recall that her father has held forth on several occasions on 'the inequality between races' in which, he maintains, he 'believes'.[13] His daughter is at pains to point out that 'republican assimilation' 'makes French people of all origins members of a single community, the national community.'[14] She pretends to regret that 'the term "national preference" has been perverted by those who want us to believe that it's a matter of racial, ethnic or religious preference.'[15] In short, she rejects all biological racism, cleverly transferring the racial and the genetic into the cultural—and even ethical and political—domain, as in the declaration that 'All the children of France have the Gauls as their ancestors, not through genetics, but through love of liberty.'[16]

In place of the anti-republican line sustained by a royalist or revolutionary section of the far right, she has substituted an ultra-republican rhetoric. She keeps her distance from the Catholic traditionalist movement, previously so influential through the mediation of its leader in the FN, Bernard Antony. She prefers to forget the fights against abortion, sex before marriage and homosexuality. Twice divorced and currently living with a man out of wedlock, she is not known for being pious or churchy. Though pointing out that her children have been baptized and taken communion, she confessed to the weekly *La Vie*: 'I am absolutely a believer, but I am a little angry with the Church. So I'm a part-time Catholic. I can't be the only one in France. I go to church for the big occasions, weddings, baptisms, Christmas and Easter.'[17] She also declared that 'priests should stay in their vestries.'[18] It was logical, then, that in 2012–13, when many FN luminaries such as Louis Aliot or Marion Maréchal-Le Pen were taking part in the 'Manif pour tous' demonstrations against proposed legislation on gay marriage, she did not make an appearance.

Some among the faithful, moreover, admit to becoming somewhat 'schizophrenic' when it comes to the Church. Wallerand de Saint-Just, party treasurer and a regional councillor for Île-de-France, is a sexagenarian with a neatly trimmed beard and pleasant manners. In his youth he was deeply involved in Catholic traditionalist politics, taking part in the occupation of the Church of Saint-Nicolas-du-Chardonnet in Paris in 1977. Today he claims to 'leave at home' his anti-abortion convictions:

> God knows how much the issue of abortion got me worked up. It's an extraordinarily important moral, human and medical question. A political official is entitled to his own obsessions, his own issues, everything that makes up a human life. But he must leave them completely to one side, become detached from that part of himself and dedicate the other part to the problems of his contemporaries. This "schizophrenia" is one

> of the hardships of a life in politics. Politicians are duty-bound to worry only about the present-day problems of their contemporaries, and so one can no longer really address issues from ten or twenty years ago such as abortion. Of course one can talk about it, but political programmes must stick to the grassroots, and as such today, to the difficulties faced by the French. That's something, notably in the FN, that our friends don't always understand. And what about gay marriage? Do the French care anymore?[19]

Of course, one may wonder whether this prudent restraint would still be the order of the day in the event of the FN taking power, and whether the ideas that its officials have 'left at home' might re-emerge without warning.

Marine Le Pen has also broken with the manly and militant tradition of the leader. Born in 1969, she is a child of the May 1968 'revolutionary' moment and of the Mitterrand years.[20] She is a modern woman, and has raised her three children. Having known life's difficulties, she speaks not only like a general to her loyal troops, but also as a woman of today to the victims of globalization's impact.

In line with a change of generation, she seems to have left behind the historic moments that constitute the French far right's memory: the 1930s and the anti-republican leagues, the Second World War and collaboration, the wars in Indochina and Algeria. Le Pen Senior had formed various movements named 'Front national' in the late 1950s and early 1960s, all linked to the defence of French Algeria.[21] His daughter has chosen hardly to mention these traumatic episodes of twentieth-century history and has erased the entire history of the French far right. As a result, veterans, profoundly influenced by such struggles, feel marginalized and keep their distance, or have left the party.[22] In the same rearrangement of ideas, Marine Le Pen has given up the fight, once fundamental to the FN of yesteryear, against the Soviet empire, communism and Marxist ideology. Her father, in a speech railing against Socialist president Mitterrand's policies in the 1980s, once thundered that the '[Soviet] model very broadly inspires in its objectives the ideology in power in our country ... Socialism and communism are the children of Marxism and their goals remain the same.'[23] Marine, in contrast, no longer wastes time attacking such 'socialo-communists' and even cites Marx in her *Pour que vive la France*.[24] Her aim is thus to attract the working-class vote, while on the international stage she is one of the most enthusiastic apologists of the Russian president Vladimir Putin, who has lamented the collapse of the USSR and who is behind a new Cold War-style anti-Washington discourse.

On various current political and geopolitical issues, she has even demonstrated a relative degree of moderation. While part of the French political class, in the face of the terrorist attacks aimed at France since 2015, insists that the national interest (*raison d'État*) should take precedence over rights and that the head of state, when necessary, should suspend constitutional law, Marine Le Pen believes that 'if the rule of law was applied properly, attacks could have been avoided. I'm not talking about a state of emergency but the rule of law.'[25] Similarly, she claims to be hostile to the 'clash of civilizations' theory formulated by the political scientist Samuel Huntington in 1993. She does not see the war between civilizational zones (notably the Islamic world and the West) as a presupposition of international politics, but as the fruit of a 'vicious globalization eager for a clash of civilizations, stultifying individuals with extremist, fundamentalist and murderous ideologies so that they forget their political consciousness and humanity!'[26] On certain points, Le Pen projects herself as less radical than some mainstream right-wing leaders and intellectuals of the 'unorthodox' right.

She also champions causes that are rarely discussed within her party, such as feminism and the environment. In a traditionally sexist and macho milieu, in which women are reduced to their role as mothers, Marine Le Pen professes a contrasting feminism. She considers herself a realistic feminist, 'constantly juggling work, shopping, children and this wretched feeling of guilt planted in the heart of every mother who each day has to solve the equation: "To bring them up, I have to earn my living—to earn my living, I have to work—if I work, it's someone other than me who's going to bring them up."'[27] But she defends women's rights because they have 'regressed'—due to the 'mass immigration and multicultural society that are setting women back centuries'.[28] In her belief that a woman 'still cannot dress how she wishes in every neighbourhood in France,' she wishes to defend a French feminism that she considers threatened by Islam and immigration, and to promote 'the image of the free and self-confident woman that our model of French culture has constructed throughout its history'.[29]

Le Pen may recruit feminism into her anti-Islam crusade, yet she violently rejects its American version, in the name of France's historical memory and above all in the name of Joan of Arc.[30] The women she celebrates are those who have contributed to the writing of 'our national novel': Geneviève, Clotilde, but also Olympe de Gouges, 'the first Frenchwoman to demand political rights for the second half of humanity', Camille Claudel, Marie Curie, and so on.[31] In her ecumenism, she mixes together activists in the modern fight for emancipation and female figures from French Catholic history. As such, the feminist struggle born in the 1960s is no longer prioritized but is accepted as a given, rather than as a fight to be fought in the future—as if there were not a vast amount still to be done in terms of equality. Rather, Le Pen's emphasis is on a consensual vision of the past, and a terrifying future. She also wishes to be heard on the question of the environment, thanks to the Nouvelle

Écologie collective, which promotes a 'patriotic ecology'. Yet the FN's environmental concerns are distinctly different from those of other ecological movements, not least in Marine Le Pen's defence of hunting, which, she says, presents no conflict with nature, since 'who knows the flora and fauna better than hunters?'[32]

In order to normalize her candidacy, Le Pen is seeking to make inroads into all sectors of society, and has created various sectoral or professional groups (*collectifs*) in milieus in which the FN traditionally has limited recruitment success. The Racine (Roots) collective aims to bring together 'patriotic teachers' in order to fight against reforms 'inspired by the permissive ideology inherited from May 1968, by aberrant pedagogical theories and by Euro-globalized dogma applied to educational policies', but also against 'an indulgent culture of excuse-making and permissiveness'.[33] The Audace (Audacity) collective is a rallying point for 'young patriotic activists' who are ready to make 'innovative and ambitious proposals, for and through those talents that wish to succeed in France'.[34] Le Pen aims to organize 'patriotic suburbs', to unite 'patriotic youth' in the Marianne collective, and even 'healthcare users'. Nothing that is human is beyond the interest of a party that wants to govern: neither culture (the Clic collective—Culture, Liberties and Creation) nor the French overseas territories (the Sea and Francophonie collective).

In the course of her 2017 presidential campaign, Le Pen was after votes everywhere, working on the ground and trying to build her influence in a range of sectors. An entire series of 'thematic conferences' was set up to enhance her presidential programme. On 7 October 2016, for instance, she attended the livestock fair at Cournon-d'Auvergne. She made sure to ground her analyses of various economic sectors in more familiar convictions. Speaking on 11 October 2016 on the theme of 'animal protection', which she strangely linked to 'human dignity' and 'respect for life, even in death', she concentrated her attacks on 'communitarian problems'. Targeting the Muslim community and abattoir procedures for so-called halal products, she underlined 'the moral requirement to stun animals before slaughtering them'. Her intervention was also aimed at humanizing her image: Florian Philippot enthused to the FN camera,'Marine adores animals!'[35] She then brought the abattoir issue into her leitmotiv of 'France at peace'—an end to ritual slaughtering would lead to 'a dying down in the level of general violence in society'—after a rather less gentle attack on Islam.

She has also broadly deployed two other themes rather overlooked by her father: the economy and secularism. This entrance into the field of economics constitutes a bid to abolish the image of a party obsessed with immigration—and the implied xenophobia behind it—but also to compete with political adversaries in terms of credibility. Though the objective of abandoning the euro scares many French people, Marine Le Pen has formulated an economic lexicon to give herself the status of an expert.[36] Nevertheless, the would-be technocratic language remains deeply informed by ideology, since this discourse takes its coherence from the struggle against 'globalism', the single source of all evils. As for secularism (*laïcité*), this is something of a novelty in a party once home to a good number of fundamentalist Catholics and anti-republican radicals, but Le Pen has taken hold of a notion that has been much discussed since the emergence of the debate about Islam's place in France.

Beyond dropping certain themes and adopting others, Marine Le Pen has also embraced a series of rhetorical tactics designed to give the impression that the FN has profoundly changed. She uses the devices previously deployed by her father as a means of avoiding charges of racism: innuendo, ellipsis, conflation, appeals to common sense and humour. She has launched a new brand of euphemization, replacing the term 'national preference' with 'national priority', which downplays the emotive idea of exclusion in favour of a positive notion of energy and entrepreneurial rigour. The FN leadership's tone is now sometimes very softened indeed; one highly placed individual in the party spoke in an interview with the author not of the 'struggle against immigration', but of 'awareness of migratory questions'. Another described his political commitment within the FN in noble and ecumenical terms: 'The idea of leading a country and of doing good to one's contemporaries is a beautiful vocation. All political officials, whatever their beliefs, have felt this moment of commitment.' Certain interviewees even reject the term 'ideology'; for Nicolas Bay, FN master of systems and elections, 'ideology consists of subjugating reality to an idea. But political struggle is all about taking realities into account. I am quite happy to fight ideology with pragmatism.'[37]

The presentation of a new discourse is very conspicuous in Le Pen's choice of references, which are extremely diverse. She has still been known to refer to far-right names such as 'the great historian Pierre Gaxotte',[38] but that was before becoming party president. She sometimes evokes Georges Bernanos—'as Bernanos said, "hope is a risk that must be run"'[39]—and another Catholic, Paul Claudel: 'there are only two things to do with the national flag: either wave it with all your might or clasp it passionately to your heart.'[40] But such pointed references have become rare, with Le Pen increasingly transgressive in the eyes of the traditional far right, particularly in her attempt to seize the Gaullist legacy. Veteran leading FN figure Bruno Gollnisch, also Marine Le Pen's unsuccessful rival for the party presidency, points out that FN activists have several reasons to detest de Gaulle:

> to strengthen his political authority he twice divided the French: first in 1944 [with the Liberation], then again in Algeria. The fact that the French Army stood aside, arms at the ready, while allowing the slaughter of

> tens of thousands of Harkis[41] who'd been assured that they wouldn't be abandoned seems to me a disgrace. De Gaulle also let the Marxists take control in the intellectual and cultural domains, which is not unconnected to the events of 1968 and François Mitterrand's victory in 1981.[42]

Yet Marine Le Pen quoted de Gaulle several times in her speech of 1 May 2011—dedicated to Joan of Arc. Later that year, she claimed the Gaullist legacy of a Europe of nations: 'As General de Gaulle put it, "To be able to end up with valid solutions, one must take account of reality. Politics is nothing other than the art of reality. And the reality is that Europe is now made up of nations."'[43] Le Pen, it seems, sees in de Gaulle her predecessor as somebody capable of lifting a country back onto its feet. Another field from which she collects her quotations—and one that jars in far-right circles—is among the luminaries of the Third Republic, and even well-known socialists. She has invoked Georges Clemenceau,[44] Jules Ferry,[45] Jean Jaurès—who, she believes, would also in his time have been 'betrayed by the left of the IMF and the chic neighbourhoods!'[46]—Émile Zola and others besides.[47]

Marine Le Pen also shows that she does not share her father's passion for history, choosing to quote from a diverse range of authors and artists who are sometimes far removed from the political. She has been known to mention the Jewish scholar and pacifist, Albert Einstein,[48] the German sociologist, Max Weber,[49] and the Surrealist and communist poet, Paul Éluard.[50] She has alluded to the Resistance poet René Char,[51] to the gay writer Jean Cocteau[52] and the left-wing philosopher Albert Camus.[53] She has referred to the left-leaning historian Marc Bloch,[54] the Jewish anti-totalitarian philosopher Hannah Arendt,[55] the anti-liberal thinker Jean-Claude Michéa[56] and the Christian theorist René Girard[57]—not forgetting the gay cinema director Luchino Visconti.[58] The important question, as we shall see, is how she uses such references—but what is certain is that Marine Le Pen has expanded to its limits her repertoire of quotations, in order to make any far-right legacy undetectable.

When she is obliged to preserve a symbol linked to far-right history, she 'republicanizes' it, as in the case of Joan of Arc, whose image was appropriated by the French far right at the beginning of the twentieth century. In her first speech as party president on 1 May 2011, on the Joan of Arc national holiday, she clarified its significance: 'On the threshold of this third millennium, one year before celebrating the six hundredth anniversary of her birth, it might appear anachronistic to be commemorating Joan of Arc. This commemoration, I would remind you, is a Republican national holiday, for Joan of Arc was both a Catholic saint and a national heroine.'[59] In other speeches she has notably quoted the historian Jules Michelet, who turned Joan of Arc into the incarnation of patriotic consciousness.[60]

While Le Pen may seek to modify her account of France's past, the far right's historical vision is polemical and anti-consensual. Many of the early FN leaders and activists were counter-revolutionaries, such as Bruno Gollnisch, who explains that he read much by authors such as Edmund Burke or Joseph de Maistre, who were philosophically opposed to the ideal of individual freedom:

> Contrary to a certain number of myths, man is not born free. There is nothing as captive as a new-born child! He is dependent on his parents. Parents thus have a natural right in educating their children. Being part of a tradition is akin to forming a chain between previous generations and those to come. I am a reactionary in the etymological sense of the term. Reaction is life![61]

Like Gollnisch, many Catholic traditionalists, Pétainists and members of Action française do not recognize themselves in the two centuries of France's republican history. Marine Le Pen's solution is to reconcile all under the banner of a renewed patriotism, proclaiming that she 'will take anything and everything' from the history of France.[62] The monarchical is thus viewed as a progression towards the Republic, and before the advent of republican universalism, she says, the country already had a vocation to export its values throughout the world: 'An ancient, splendid land, which through centuries of history had forged and radiated those universal values that it was to choose for its motto: liberty, equality, fraternity.'[63] She then brings together historical figures traditionally contrasted by the far right: 'From Clovis [king of the Franks] to General de Gaulle, by way of Joan of Arc, yes, of course, Joan of Arc! All the great names of our history have built France, have all given of their best to take part in this collective adventure.'[64] Again, she evokes 'this eternal France which stretches from Alesia to the referendum of 2005',[65] wanting to restore a 'national story' that she believes to have been defiled by her political adversaries.[66]

Finally, to pre-empt the usual accusations of indulgence towards wartime collaboration—from which a large part of the French far right emerged—Marine Le Pen has offered a neat reversal of roles, whereby the FN inherits the legacy of resistance against the Nazi occupier, while the political class were the collaborators. Pointing to the alliance between Burgundy and England in Joan of Arc's time, she remarks that 'the Burgundians were *collabos*', while those who defended national sovereignty embody 'Free France'.[67] She is fond of recalling that 'France built herself on a spirit of resistance, on values of courage and honour which, each time that she has been threatened in her history, have allowed her to stand tall again and to continue her glorious march forwards. France has known a day like 11 November 1940 [a demonstration against the German occupation by high school and university students], and she will know others like it, for she will never submit.'[68] As for Nicolas Sarkozy, president at the time of this speech, he 'doesn't like France, and every day he collaborates a little more with his masters: the markets and the banks. He is always quick to align our country with someone else, the US one day, Germany the next.'[69]

Marine Le Pen's Front National, then, has adopted several tactics to exonerate itself from its past and distance itself from the losing side of history—counter-revolutionaries and anti-secularizers at the end of the nineteenth century, anti-republicans in the 1930s, collaborators in the 1940s, supporters of colonization and anti-Gaullists in the 1950s and 1960s. Louis Aliot works hard on this, even denying the existence of an integral ideology in the party: 'There isn't an FN ideology. Its ideas are fluid. Jean-Marie Le Pen invented, without knowing it at the start, an attitude, a form of behaviour, a political positioning which led him to create not a school of thought, but a political movement that has endured and which now carries weight in public opinion. But its sources are many and various.'[70] He believes that all the incriminations directed at the FN in an attempt to place it within the ideological history of the far right are unfair, and that any such blame should be apportioned just as much, if not more, to the left.

He claims that the FN was not born out of collaboration, but out of the problematic past of colonization and French Algeria:

> the history of colonization has been just as much—and in the beginning more—a history of the left as of the right. If you reread the speeches of Jules Ferry, they were colonialist and even racialist. You had to bring light to colonized peoples, that's what he wrote! Colonialism was born on the left, and it was only later that it was defended by what people call the far right.' As for collaboration, 'it's said that it started with Marshal Pétain. Yet all of Pétain's entourage started on the left: Déat, Doriot, Laval ... and many others. Resistance fighters were partly recruited from among the far right, Action française's [far-right youth organization] Camelots du Roi, for example. Anti-Semitism cannot be systematically attached to the far right alone, because the left is also involved. Michel Onfray insists that anti-Semitism was a powerful factor in the thinking of Proudhon and even Marx. And de Gaulle, too, is not beyond blame, when he spoke of Jews as 'a confident and dominant people'. Anyway, he was a traditional Catholic military officer and had little to say on the subject, even during the war.[71]

In short, according to Aliot, all allegations levelled against his political family should above all be directed at the left. Through a strategy of obfuscation, it is thus possible also to accuse the left of what is alleged against the far right, by deliberately confusing the issue.

It is essential to look back to the FN's ideological trajectory to assess whether today's party really has nothing to do with the history of the far right. The issue is extremely sensitive, especially because of the father's racist outbursts and the daughter's intention to accede to power, as admitted by party treasurer Wallerand de Saint-Just: 'Any clumsy or unfortunate phrase can kill us. And Marine Le Pen is all too aware of it.'[72] Leaving aside soundbites and declarations about 'detoxification', we must drill down into Le Pen's themes, arguments, quotations and references, to find the ideological motifs she constructs from speech to speech.

Jean-Marie Le Pen's vision of the world is a pseudo-scientific version of the far right's time-honoured thinking, although he uses racial 'science' less than demography and a historical model of sociology to explain that the Western world has fallen into a state of decadence—because of the end of religion and the emancipation of women, with the ensuing demographic decline—and that it must henceforth fight to survive in the face of successive migratory invasions. Marine Le Pen does not identify with this sort of scientific tropism, clearly sensing that her father's way of thinking has little impact on society as it remains too abstract and eccentric to be credible, appealing only to a marginal group of self-appointed specialists in demographic and migratory movements. The new FN president has instead chosen another all-encompassing explanation for the current state of the world, one that is more popularly accessible and a great deal more appealing. According to her, we, in our developed and relatively prosperous countries, live under a hitherto unknown form of totalitarianism, in which a power as invisible as it is absolute has been taking hold over several decades. Through a duplicitous media, the hegemony of advertising and marketing, the tyranny of consumption, Internet surveillance and a standardized political discourse, the French, she claims, have been transformed into brainless consumers.

Such an intuition is no doubt attractive to many, and Marine Le Pen lends it unusual emphasis. From this basis, from this grand vision of a subjugated world, she can then develop in coherent terms the three principal thrusts of the new FN's thinking. Firstly, confronted with a Republic emptied of its meaning because of its ineffectiveness, she advocates its reconstruction, starting from the people and the state. Then, in reaction to a political life artificially divided between a left and a right that, a few nuances aside, apply the same programme, she claims to transcend the left/right dichotomy. Finally, in a party where xenophobia has always played a major role, she retains a subliminal type of racism. Her very violent utterances against 'globalized elites' look back to the social anti-Semitism of the nineteenth century, while her artfully subtle attacks on Islam provide her with a new scapegoat. Within the totalitarian schema that she has set up, the economic elites have decided to use cheap migrant labour, casting true Frenchmen and Frenchwomen into poverty and onto society's margins. Marine Le Pen, in formulating her worldview, has found allies, most notably Vladimir Putin,[73] in her struggle against the principal manipulator of this new totalitarianism, the European and American order. We'll now see how she makes use of this worldview.

4

A TOTALITARIAN UNIVERSE

Jean-Marie Le Pen used to fight against Soviet totalitarianism, which collapsed in 1991. His daughter feels herself to be involved in an even more grandiose struggle, against an insidious form of totalitarianism that seeks to impose itself upon all of us today. The FN president often summarizes her party's ideology in terms of a struggle against two unprecedented forms of totalitarianism: Islamism and globalism.[1] The first is considered 'all-religious', the second 'all-financial'.[2] The term 'totalitarianism' refers primarily to Nazism and Stalinism, but it has been often applied to regimes such as Mao's in China or, more recently, to North Korea or Turkmenistan. It implies not only the individual's submission to the state, but also absolute control, the unconditional mobilization of an entire society and the creation of a perfectly malleable 'new man'. Nowadays this notion is used by a handful of intellectuals, albeit rarely, to characterize liberal societies or the techno-scientific or consumerist universe.[3]

The challenge clearly lies in daring to compare our societies with the Nazi and Stalinist regimes, since it is difficult to assimilate our social systems, despite all their forms of alienation, into the total ideological control and murderous terror that accompany totalitarian regimes. Yet Marine Le Pen has no hesitation in taking up such a notion and giving it surprising prominence, for her entire vision of humanity in today's world is guided by this hypothesis of totalitarianism. Islamism, she believes, remains both an external and internal threat to France, but one which has not yet prevailed. Globalism, on the other hand, constitutes a force that effectively subjugates every democracy. As such, she presents herself as the only adversary of this globalist totalitarianism, a complete and yet elusive power that weighs on our bodies and minds. By what stages, starting with a critique of liberal Europe, has she arrived at this idea of the zombification of humanity?

The argument starts with the political and the economic, aimed at the European Union, which Marine Le Pen has selected as one of her main targets. The EU, she claims, is responsible for the decline in purchasing power following the introduction of the euro and also for France's loss of sovereignty. She has thus supported the idea of France leaving the eurozone and, following the UK's 'yes' vote on Brexit, has demanded a referendum on France's membership of the EU, or 'Frexit'. Her grievances are firstly pragmatic: Europe is inefficient and the 'dogma' of the euro 'is increasingly failing in the eyes of the whole world as more and more economists are ready to acknowledge'.[4] Against 'absurd and suicidal policies', 'France will return to the fold of independent nations thanks to monetary freedom!'[5]

Europe, moreover, is perceived as anti-democratic: 'the Europe of Brussels has been built on denying or bypassing the will of the people,'[6] insists Le Pen, an MEP. Believing that the democratic process is only possible within a national framework,[7] she insists that there is no choice but to 'throw off the shackles of a stifling and destructive Brussels, which holds us against our will and deprives us of all room for manoeuvre in whole areas of political action: currency, legislation, control of our borders, the management of immigration...'[8] Marine Le Pen attributes the inefficiency and tyranny of Europe to a Kafkaesque bureaucracy with many failings: anonymity, red tape, protocol, absurd decision-making, ideological conformism, distance from the people, opaqueness and connivance with various economic lobbies and powers. Bureaucracy—alongside, of course, an absence of democracy—is often considered one of the distinctive characteristics of a totalitarian society.[9] Thus she clearly depicts the European project as totalitarian: 'The French state has been put at the service of the Brussels bureaucracy, which bypasses the noble idea of European harmony and puts in its place a project that is technocratic, totalitarian and harmful to our freedoms.'[10]

Totalitarianism is not just based on a ruling caste but also depends on a broader and more extensive superstructure, which Marine Le Pen views as an anonymous 'order' or a 'dogma', an ideology blissfully accepted by all due to a cunning propaganda process. The 'European techno-structure' is thus 'subservient to the financial markets, totally removed from the people'. These financial actors, she says, are 'the order of the market which makes its own laws'[11] and which 'fires managers and puts bankers in positions of power in countries like Greece or Italy'.[12] Most importantly, the true leaders are neither commissioners nor heads of state, since Europe in truth 'takes its orders from Goldman Sachs'.[13] This perspective—even if Le Pen denies any accusation of conspiratorialism[14]—encourages conspiracy theorists convinced that a world order made up of the financial (and Jewish, in the anti-Semitic versions) elite is seeking to dominate the planet. For them, power is never where one believes it to reside, and today's totalitarianism is phantasmal.

Le Pen often uses religious vocabulary when referring to support for European political union ('Europeanist dogma'),[15] for the single currency ('euro dogma')[16] and for economic liberalism ('the dogma of ultraliberalism and laissez-faireism').[17] But these are not tenets of a true religion; rather, they represent an archaic faith, a pagan devotion to an idol demanding its sacrifices. The aim of Europeanist ideology is hence 'to impose on exhausted peoples everywhere in Europe new sacrifices designed to preserve the sacred dogma of our Europeanist elites, the golden calf of the euro, and to enrich even further ... the pro-market order.'[18] The religion of rootless elites is to be seen as a cruel and sectarian dogma, far removed from evangelical values. The 'Europeanists', it follows, have transformed money, which is 'just an instrument! Nothing more!',[19] 'into a sort of divinity that must be adored for its own sake. Some worship a guru or a demiurge, others amongst us worship the euro! The sect of euro worshippers!'[20] Manipulating people as the priests of old shepherded children, the advocates of the euro seek 'these days to terrify our compatriots. They are reduced to a terrible state of anxiety by being constantly told that if the euro disappears, it will be the cataclysm. That if the euro were to disappear, it would even be the end of the world!'[21] Marine Le Pen beseeches her fellow citizens to escape this religious terror, created and maintained by a controlling caste.

This discourse denouncing the financial order is accompanied by the denunciation of another totalitarianism that moulds minds: globalism. Here, Marine Le Pen remains doubly faithful to her father, since the term *mondialisme* was used by the latter[22] from 1984, and especially after 1995—while the neo-fascist and revolutionary ultra-right has used it since the 1960s.[23] Jean-Marie Le Pen made the struggle against Soviet totalitarianism one of his favourite themes; she, like him, can claim to be a fighter against the same evil. Recycling an old metaphor describing the Soviet empire, she has applied the term 'prison of the peoples' to the EU.[24] Yet if the EU is the new USSR, Marine is at pains to point out that communism is no longer the enemy:

> The right/left logic, the socialism/liberalism logic that has prevailed up to now with its paroxysm in 1981 has been replaced by another contrast of opposites. ... The collapse of the Wall and the shipwreck of communism, the ideological rallying of the socialists to ultraliberalism and capitalist deregulation have hardened this new dichotomy, that which now opposes in a fundamental and implacable way supporters of the nation state against globalists. ... Globalists from right and left quite openly cherish the plan for a universal empire governed by the laws... of the market. Behind the ethereal myth of a world without enemies, and of a happiness that they can only imagine as materialistic, hides an unrelenting ideology, a totalitarian ideology, a market-based ideology whose monstrous project is one of a planet in thrall to consumption and production for the benefit of a few big businesses or banks which alone stand to profit.[25]

For Le Pen, globalism is much more than an 'economic system' or a 'technical phenomenon'. It is an 'ideology that far exceeds mere globalization and which aims to standardize cultures, to encourage nomadism, the permanent movement of uprooted people from one continent to another, to make them interchangeable and, in essence, to render them anonymous.'[26] She explains, dizzyingly, how this invisible power looks to 'empty from our heads' the notion that 'nations' and 'cultures' can be 'over-full' or swamped. Globalism consists of 'the alliance between consumerism and materialism, in order to forcibly remove Man from History and cast him into what Gilles Lipovetsky calls "the era of emptiness".'[27] She believes that the seizure of power from nations by economic liberalism is paralleled by a discourse seeking to turn individuals into zombies. This new opium of the masses transforms 'the forgotten, the invisible, the anonymous, from whom all identity must be withdrawn' into 'amorphous and obedient consumers, servile in the face of the advertising and commercial orders issued by CAC 40 corporations.'[28] Whereas totalitarianism is traditionally linked to the omnipotence of the state—fascist, Nazi or Soviet—Le Pen situates it within a diffuse and gentle form of power, emerging from the sphere of globalized capitalism.

From speech to speech, she has listed the reasons for her anti-totalitarianism, bringing together the most classical and contemporary of references. The FN wants to guarantee Internet freedom—as part of a struggle against 'a totalitarian attempt to impose surveillance and stalking on Internet users, something that even Orwell's Big Brother couldn't have dreamt of and the obvious goal of which is to try to silence that dissidence, that ferment of intelligence, that has sought refuge on the web.'[29] Taking advantage of the wave of protest caused by Snowden affair in 2013, which revealed the extent of US digital surveillance across the world, Le Pen denounced 'a world where we see the generalized surveillance of all for the benefit of a few, like in the worst works of fiction.'[30] Attempting to persuade her readers that a psycho-power more efficient than that of the old totalitarian regimes is falling into place, she again quoted the author of *1984*: 'Power over matter—external reality, as you would call it—is not important. Already our control over matter is absolute ... We control matter because we control the mind. Reality is inside the skull.'[31] This goes much further than condemning the power of the media, as her father did regularly; Marine Le Pen is seeking to denounce a much more ambitious brainwashing phenomenon.

Another ingredient in this vision of totalitarianism is the nightmare of a supranational state run by a small circle of anonymous individuals, and here again the EU is no more than a front: 'The Europeanist monster being built in Brussels, which defines itself, in a semantic fraud, as "Europe", is nothing less than a conglomerate under American protection, the antechamber of a total, global world state.'[32] In this context, she is keen to cite one of her *bêtes noires*, Jacques Attali,[33] who has declared himself in favour of global governance.[34] Removing any nuances from such an intellectual hypothesis, here Le Pen is in the realm of countless conspiracy theories circulating on the Internet concerning a supposed world government.

Totalitarian systems, whether in the USSR or Nazi Germany, have taken care to control their youth so as to shape future humanity. According to an alarmed Marine Le Pen, a similar process is underway within the French state education system: 'Help! SOS Racisme and other propaganda organizations are permanently in place in the very heart of our children's schools. That is how the System hopes to indoctrinate and condition future voters. Farewell to neutrality! Farewell to secularism! Welcome, propaganda! Welcome, brainwashing!'[35] The dream of creating a new man, freed of the weight of the past and completely malleable, has structured forms of fascism as well as Soviet and Chinese communism, and Le Pen maintains that globalism has now taken up this demiurgic project: 'The European Union intends to fashion a new man, uniform in his tastes and progressively torn away from his national culture.'[36]

The first, destructive stage consists of an uprooting process: 'dilution of the Nation, weakening of the family, disappearance of national solidarity, negation of our identity and roots, erasing our memory, scorn towards values of effort, work, merit, courage, righteousness.'[37] The authors of this speech certainly drew inspiration from the philosopher Hannah Arendt's trilogy *The Origins of Totalitarianism*, in which Arendt explains that totalitarianism has been able to take root due to the emergence of 'atomized masses'. The individual bonds all the more easily with the state as he feels freed from forms of social solidarity, such that men have been moulded to blindly follow the orders of the state. Hence, 'Terror can rule absolutely only over men who are isolated against one another.'[38] This isolation, in the totalitarian system, becomes loneliness—in other words, 'the experience of not belonging to the world at all, which is among the most radical and desperate experiences of man.'[39] Having destroyed social classes, political parties, civil society and families, the totalitarian state does as it wishes with individuals: 'To be uprooted means to have no place in the world recognized and guaranteed by others; to be superfluous means not to belong to the world at all. Uprootedness can be the preliminary condition for superfluousness, just as isolation can (but must not) be the preliminary condition for loneliness.'[40] Thus Marine Le Pen offers an identity-based reading of Arendt, who was herself unfamiliar with any nostalgic vision of rootedness in an old order.

Le Pen has also combined this interpretation with typically right-wing considerations such as the loss of 'collective memory'[41] or the end of hierarchy: 'The teacher is the equal of the student, the policeman of the delinquent.'[42] Based on a vision of an uprooted, lonely and manipulable humanity, and building on the social theme of defending 'the forgotten',[43] she introduces the metaphysical concept of the 'interchangeable' man. At the opening of her presidential campaign in the village of Brachay on 3 December 2016, she announced:

> Our project is based on rejecting individualism and the power of money, on refusing to subject mankind to a purely consumerist logic carried out by greedy multina-

tionals who would turn the individual into an interchangeable being, a being whose only raison d'être is to produce and consume—or be unemployed.

This idea is borrowed from *L'Identité malheureuse* by the controversial philosopher Alain Finkielkraut,[44] for whom the purely economic calculation that 'the influx of immigrants providentially compensates for the falling birth-rate on the Old Continent' overlooks the reality of identity issues. Thus, 'experience tells us that individuals are not interchangeable', that 'true Frenchmen' cannot be replaced with strangers without there being a price to pay. Finkielkraut, in turn, has taken this idea from his reading of Charles Péguy (1873–1914), who developed the theory of a 'universal interchangeability' imposed by money's rule over societies.[45] This notion, then, contains an intrinsic critique of a world dominated by calculations of interest and profit. Péguy, regularly quoted by Marine Le Pen, is one of France's most original writers and also one of the inspirations for those who lament the moral mediocrity of the modern bourgeoisie. She follows this line of thought when she declares: 'Division is born out of individualism and "me first", out of the instant gratification of material desires through money' 'in this "all-financial" society where everything is to be bought or sold.'[46] The idea of interchangeability is also employed by writers firmly situated on the far right. Renaud Camus, author of the 'Great Replacement' theory, condemns a 'culture of idiocy':

> If you want me to say that major international financial interests require for their business a replaceable, interchangeable, decultured, dehumanized, robotized humankind, I will say it very willingly, and in all sincerity. Some implicate the American empire, others Europe, the Jews, freemasons, Bilderberg, the Trilateral Commission, and so on. And perhaps each of these entities does carry some responsibility.[47]

The rhetoric of the individual's 'replaceability' (by migrants or by the misery of consumerism) allows Marine Le Pen to revisit the old fantasy—given new currency since recent advances in robotics—of machines replacing people. According to her, 'machines are becoming the equals of men, who as a result are treated like machines',[48] within an organized system of 'modern-day slavery' in which 'debt' and 'stock market-led redundancies'[49] produce a disposable worker.

Completing her vision of a contemporary form of totalitarianism, Marine Le Pen has made her own the theme of safeguarding the real against the virtualization of the world,[50] through which globalism seeks to disconnect the life of a country and its people from reality. Criticizing France's surrender of sovereignty to Europe and big business, she pillories an imagined enemy: 'Having dreamt of an economy without factories, Euro-globalism has ended up wanting to impose the idea of a country without people.'[51] What 'the Caste' wants to do is to 'hold sway without the people, even against the people. No group, no sector can escape it. Even having fun in public is an inconvenience. We live in a sanitized world where rubbish trucks are sent to put an end to street events.'[52] This world 'where the people's happiness is measured by the extent of their consumption'[53] is totally intertwined with a set of norms and proscriptions aimed at cleansing it of its traditional impurities.

As for nations, they are to be reduced to 'mere geographical spaces', zones of exploitation and consumption. Inspired by the vision of France offered by Michel Houellebecq at the end of his novel *The Map and the Territory* (*La Carte et le territoire*), Marine Le Pen becomes indignant:

> Nor do I want [France] to become a tourist theme park for a few weeks in the summer. I don't want her to become a vast Disneyland to entertain dazed children with her so-called conserved nature. I don't want her to become an Indian reservation where the last peasants will have become landscape gardeners. The soil fertilized by our ancestors, the towns built through centuries of effort deserve better than the fate of becoming frozen, motionless, fossilized museum pieces.[54]

This habit of bemoaning a France turned into a museum by tourism, the cultural policies of the Mitterrand era, local festivals, multimedia libraries and regional folklorism is nothing new; it is a recurring idea among many far-right polemicists.[55] In reaction to the virtualization of the world, she promises: 'I will be ... the president of a return to the real ...! Stuck in its bubble, which like all speculative bubbles is bound one day to burst, the Caste has lost all contact with the real. The world that it imposes on us, which is its world, has nothing to do with ours, the real one. Its world is virtual.'[56] Marine Le Pen quotes the French philosopher Jean Baudrillard,[57] who explores the theme of the definitive victory of the simulacrum or sham over reality[58]—and who has no connection to the far right.

She is much closer to Aleksandr Dugin, co-founder of the National Bolshevik Party in 1992 and one of the best-known Russian theoreticians of Neo-Eurasianism, an anti-Western doctrine merging thought from the National Bolshevik movement and the New Right. Admired within European far-right milieus, he paints a picture of the triumph of liberalism similar to that presented by Marine Le Pen. It is known that Dugin visits France regularly and that he is in touch with various members of the FN. It is likely, then, that Le Pen's speechwriters will be familiar with the French translations of his works. He offers a hyperbolic nightmare vision of globalism's intrusion into the collective consciousness: 'Having overcome its adversaries, liberalism has acquired a monopoly in ideological thought, it has become the only ideology and allows no other. One could say that it has passed from the level of programme to a working system, that it has become something taken for granted.'[59] It has even passed from 'the level of discourse to that of language': 'unconscious, incorporated, instinctive'.[60] The main consequence of this process is loss of contact with what is real, as liberalism must take over our minds in order to 'sell' us all possible metamorphoses, and because the resulting detachment offers the prospect of unending malleability:

> The logic of global liberalism and globalization draws us towards the abyss of postmodern dissolution in the virtual. Our youth already has one foot in this abyss: the codes of global liberalism insinuate themselves with increasing efficiency on the level of the unconscious, in habits, advertising, glamour, technologies, networking models. Loss of identity, not only national or cultural but also sexual and, soon, human, is now commonplace.[61]

Contemporary phenomena such as the digitalisation of everyday life, new forms of algorithm-based Internet marketing, recognition of gay rights and transhumanism are all viewed as part of an apocalyptic tableau, the final stage in globalism's takeover of our age.

Yet Le Pen's discourse is also proactive, since she presents herself as the best hope of resisting totalitarianism; she proposes several weapons with which to fight the homogenization allegedly imposed by liberalism. The first of these is political and can be summed up by her manifesto: return to the franc, a referendum on France's future in the EU, the policy of 'national priority'. She justifies her essentially protectionist and xenophobic policies with a metaphysical notion of the world's diversity, emphatically celebrating 'the diversity and, indeed, the radiance of the world, free from the flavourless mush of one-dimensional globalism which is the opposite of the universal'.[62] Defending the world's diversity was one of the leading ideas of the think tank GRECE (Research and Study Group for European Civilization), one of the main strands of the New Right to appear in the late 1960s, whose aims included laying claim to 'cultural hegemony'.[63] According to the precepts of the Italian Marxist philosopher Antonio Gramsci (1891–1937), before exercising power over political society it is indispensable to take possession of civil society—to win its heart and mind. If the FN ever comes to power in France, it will owe its success in part to the New Right, even if these 'Gramscians of the right' refuse to play the game of politics and assert their intellectual independence.

One of GRECE's historic characteristics was its interest in studying Indo-European societies, and its promotion of paganism against a Christianity viewed as assimilated with 'the ideology of Sameness'.[64] Advocacy of paganism—which implies a cyclical conception of history, rejection of the virtues of compassion and of the idea of a chosen people, and opposition to unitary universalism—clears the way for the notion of difference as a central concept. Such a construct can then be translated into 'ethno-differentialism', opposition to the idea of ethnic mixing. In the name of an ideal that has attracted many of her contemporaries,[65] Marine Le Pen places the rejection of immigrants and Muslims under the noble banner of respecting difference, insisting that 'the world will only survive through human and cultural diversity, through biodiversity'.[66] And yet the only difference that matters is that between the 'French way of life' and the wider world. Immigrants are therefore firmly asked to assimilate totally, or to leave. According to specialists on 'the Front National's networks',[67] it is precisely individuals previously associated with GRECE 'who provided [Le Pen] with the basis of such arguments (from which she has careful erased any remaining paganism): if globalization is a system designed to destroy peoples, the real schism is no longer between right and left, but between the "globalists", in other words those who intend to ban "national identity", and their enemies.'[68]

For Aleksandr Dugin, a fightback is also possible: 'Only a crusade against the United States, the West, globalization and their theological-ideological liberalism, can constitute an adequate response. ... The production of this crusade's ideology is incontestably Russia's task, not alone but in concert with all world forces that resist, in one way or another, "the American century". In all cases, moreover, this ideology must start by recognizing the fatal role of liberalism in pervading the West, from the moment that it rejected the values of God and Tradition.'[69] The FN, an open ally of Vladimir Putin's Russia in its struggle against the West, is an active participant in this ideological struggle. Putin himself, in his speech to the Valdai Discussion Club on 27 October 2016, expressed his view of what he perceived as a revolt of the Western masses, against their rulers in the United States, France or the rest of Europe: as a decisive weapon in his fight against the West.[70]

The other tactic to be used in the battle against globalism is the restoration of traditional forms of solidarity, an idea given considerable emphasis by Marine Le Pen. In her desire to combat the individualism and isolation caused by the ethos of consumption,[71] she intends to 'put the collective back at the centre of our values'.[72] Again referring to George Orwell, she has highlighted the 'common decency' of the ordinary people, so far removed from the supposedly scandalous and obscene behaviour of the financial, media and political elites.[73] For Orwell, far from totalitarian newspeak, the common people maintain a powerful rapport with what is real and embody, without proclaiming it, a day-to-day moral code of selflessness, friendship and honour that he termed common decency.[74] As the self-proclaimed candidate of the people, Le Pen gives Orwell's words a French resonance, basing 'love for a country and a people, passion for a language and feeling for a history and for those little everyday things that make us who we are' on 'an affective and popular connection'.[75] Against the arrogance of the elites, the chicanery of the financiers, media manipulation, the brainwashing of marketing, liberal exploitation and the advertising-led standardization of behaviour, she contrasts a popular, modest and reasonable wisdom, convivial and rooted in community.

The idea of this struggle against a totalitarianism that has become invisible and global is not just Marine Le Pen's personal obsession, but is central to the party line as a whole. The learned Nicolas Bay is also convinced that we live under a totalitarian regime: 'When they hear the word "totalitarianism", people automatically think of the murderous regimes of the twentieth century. But today we have a new form of it with a subjugation of the individual that comes especially through the power of the media and new technologies. One sees it in social networks, which are a formidable tool for freedom but which at the same time are used so that people remain isolated in front of their computers, alone and without social life, vulnerable, in the grasp of a consumerist society. A materialist logic exists in suppressing social bonds. We're convinced that we have 150 friends on Facebook, but in reality we haven't got a single one anymore because we no longer see or talk to them. Even business is affected by this disintegration through remote working, which—if it becomes commonplace—leads to the disappearance of social ties through virtualization. Attacks on freedom take many forms: assaults on sovereignty, which is the freedom to defend our borders and to choose our own destiny; on individual liberties through the state of emergency and intelligence legislation; on the freedoms of car owners through so-called environmental protection and expensive fuel; or on "digital freedoms". A totalitarian regime is in the process of being built.'[76] The FN's slogan for the 2017 presidential election was, of course, 'freedom'.

Whether this vision of things is a caricature or the stuff of fantasy matters little to Marine Le Pen, since she has made this theory, confusedly shared by part of society, the foundation of her ideology. This philosophical stance gives her propositions, now based on an ambitious and coherent view of the world, a solidity that her father's FN could never attain. Against this anti-totalitarian background, she can now line up three new policy axes: a re-evaluation of republicanism, a self-definition as 'neither right nor left', and the identification of new enemies within.

5

THE REPUBLICAN TURN

'So, yes, my dear friends, I proclaim it bluntly: we are profoundly republican, profoundly and sincerely attached to the pillars of our collective pact, to the fundamental values that France has chosen, to the founding principles on which she is built.' On 1 May 2013, standing in front of Joan of Arc's statue in Paris, Marine Le Pen was determined to prove her good faith when she expressed her unconditional support for the Republic. She had already, in her investiture speech as party president on 16 January 2011, made herself clear: the FN 'has shown that it is certainly a great republican political party. ... Who has defended these principles better than us in the course of forty years of French political history? Nobody, in truth, for these principles have been at the heart of our movement's DNA from its start. Who today can sustain these principles better than the Front National?' And yet the return of the Republic and its values to the FN's discourse was not entirely Marine Le

Pen's work; her father had made this about-turn during the 2007 presidential election campaign. Under the influence of his daughter and the anti-Semitic polemicist Alain Soral, he made his 'Valmy speech', which celebrated the people up in arms saving the nation in 1792. But this late conversion was not entirely credible, and so it fell to his daughter to oversee the party's return to the republican fold.

The stakes are high. For decades the FN has been spurned by a large part of the political class, with certain politicians ruling out any form of alliance and establishing a 'cordon sanitaire' around it. It is true that the party, with its leagues, royalists and revolutionary nationalists, was born of a movement that often fought against the Republic and democracy. From the interwar slogan 'crève la gueuse'[1] to the military putsch in Algeria, via Pétain's French state, the desire to overthrow the Republic has been a recurrent one. In his *Rivarol* of 9 April 2015, Jean-Marie Le Pen spoke directly and angrily to anti-republican voters: 'And then the way [Socialist Prime Minister] Valls[2] keeps referring to the Republic! They're all starting to bore me with their Republic!'

The majority of French people are also still fearful of the FN. In February 2016, 56 per cent of those questioned in an annual field survey considered that the FN represented a danger, against 38 per cent who thought the opposite.[3] More than half of those polled associated the FN with a risk to the values, and even the existence, of democracy and the Republic. This perception has so far kept Marine Le Pen's FN from victory in major electoral contests. Though its vote share has increased at each election, until the April 2017 presidentials it had considerable difficulty reaching the second round of voting.[4] So what more can she do, having already tried to transform the FN's rhetoric and even its political positioning? Apart from the declared rejection of anti-Semitism and biological racism, Marine Le Pen and her advisers have decided to move into the field of the Republic and the values that are attached to it: democracy, nation, state. But they give a very particular meaning to these concepts.

The first tactic is for Le Pen to lay claim to France's revolutionary heritage and the original values of the Republic, in order to proclaim herself the candidate of the people. Taking notions connected to the history of the Revolution and reinterpreting them—in her own way—she suggests that today's France has reverted to the *ancien régime*, whereby the people are ignored and the general interest overlooked, defeated by 'the feudalisms of finance, politics, religion or the mafia'.[5] Hence her implicit call for a revolution that would abolish once again the system of privileges. The same symbolism is deployed when she seeks to enumerate the grievances of the rural population, whom she likens to a Third Estate dominated by the aristocracy of globalized elites.[6] Le Pen also extols the republican value of liberty; as Cécile

Alduy and Stéphane Wahnich suggest, freedom is primarily understood in her speeches as independence from external influences, and as sovereignty.[7] The French people demonstrate their collective freedom when they refuse to give in to the injunctions of a foreign country, the EU, other international organizations, the globalized economy or economic liberalism. For Le Pen, the apogee of France's freedom in recent years was the country's rejection of a European constitution in 2005.[8] She has similarly developed the revolutionary theme of the nation in danger.[9]

The second tactic is to call for a reconstruction of the Republic, which she believes has been emptied of its meaning, and to this end the FN's leader invokes another pillar of the national motto: equality. This concept has often been attacked by the far right, which tends to support the pre-eminence of a natural hierarchical order, but according to Marine Le Pen, it is the elites of the 'global hyper-class' who have created a new form of inegalitarianism, and broken the republican pact by favouring immigrants to the detriment of national citizens. In order to restore equality, she thus proposes several preliminary objectives:

> Unlike other parties, we do not think it is adequate to affirm one's attachment to such values, but that one must give those values the conditions essential to their existence. ... We believe in the equality of French citizens, whatever their origins or beliefs. That is why we

> will not tolerate it when certain people who enter our territory are *more equal than others*. When certain people, entering illegally, unlawfully into our land, have *more rights than the French themselves*.[10]

These vague arguments—it is not, in fact, the case that foreigners, especially illegal immigrants, benefit from more rights than French citizens—suggest that the breaking of the republican pact stems from an inequality introduced by non-citizens. The Republic, Le Pen believes, will only be reconstructed when foreigners are removed from the system of French rights. However, in the present-day Republic, it is unconstitutional for legal migrants to be excluded from the social security system, or deprived of access to employment in the private sector.[11] Le Pen, therefore, is seeking an anti-republican course of action in order to give birth to 'her' republic.

Her third tactic consists of declaring herself more democratic than her opponents. The main argument in favour of a republic that excludes foreigners is that it would express the will of the people: 'We want to be able to decide in our country what is good for us. It's simple, and it's been the very essence of democracy for millennia, since Ancient Greece.'[12] Marine Le Pen considers that the voice of the people is unheard because states live under the diktat of an economic liberalism that controls politics and stifles democracy: 'Globalism is a profoundly anti-democratic ideology.'[13] She is equally critical of the majority vote system that deprives the FN of proportional representation, declaring that 'direct democracy is the best form of government, above all because it allows citizens, members of the same community, to be involved in decisions, in participation with complete sovereignty.'[14] Far from supporting experimental local democracy or Internet voting, she is in favour of multiple referendums:

> As often as is necessary, I will use popular consultation to decide the great questions debated by the nation, because I believe in collective intelligence, and we are paid to know that the French people are ... the ones who know what's best for the French people![15]

In the event of winning the 2017 presidential election, she had planned several referendums in order to revise the Constitution,[16] and had also promised to consult the French population on leaving the European Union. Rather than a reinvention of democratic procedure, this strategy amounts to bypassing the election of representatives through direct appeals to the people, thereby risking further social division.

The fourth 'republican' tactic lies in extolling a strong state, since for Le Pen 'the state is key.'[17] On this issue, the break with the past is significant, given the degree of previous attacks on the economic concept of the state by an openly Poujadist,[18] anti-Soviet and anti-socialist FN.[19] Here the influence of recent FN recruits drawn from a statist sort of *chevènementisme*,[20] notably Florian Philippot, appears crucial. Le Pen has identified a solution to the chaotic dominance of economic liberalism, and will subordinate nation, democracy and Republic to it:

> Without a strong state there is no security, and without authority there is no security. ... It is that strong state that through the centuries has managed to unite the Nation, contain feudal and communitarian conflict, destroy tribalism, develop our territory and gradually offer to all an education, healthcare, security and excellent public services.[21]

Pondering the purpose of the state, she concludes that it was created

> in order to wrest human life from violence! Yes, my dear compatriots, violence, which alas is primordial in a state of nature and which must be subdued to prise men and women, above all the weakest, away from acts of power, raw power, guaranteeing enough peace and public security for the individual to come and go and to flourish.[22]

The argument, and even the vocabulary, comes from the political philosophy of Thomas Hobbes, who proposed in the seventeenth century that the only way to avoid a 'war of all against all' was for each individual to delegate his or her capacity for self-defence to a state, the Leviathan, which would then possess the necessary strength to put down any inclination towards disorder. The security of all obviously comes with a price: the omnipotence of the state, which nobody has the right or means to resist. It is such a Leviathan-state that Marine

Le Pen seems to invoke, using the warlike concept of 'the state as strategist', a state that must impose its will upon the individual as well as civil society, associations, NGOs and so on.

Le Pen's discourse on the state, it should be noted, has created some tension within the various far-right currents in France today. Indeed, it is accompanied by what amounts to an ode to unification: 'The French people are the result of fifteen centuries, at least, of a slow and patient work of unification.'[23] It stands against regionalist tendencies nurtured today by 'identitarians' who, from Lille to Nice, promote notions of local identity, European civilization and hatred of Islam. If Le Pen sometimes gives support locally to the 'identitarian' movement,[24] ultimately she favours a centralizing state. If she became president, she promised, 'local feudal structures, in the regions and departments, will be fought. Democracy can express itself at the local level. But it is inconceivable that the executives of our communities can turn themselves into so many petty lordships.'[25] The state will correct a 'decentralization process that is now out of control'.[26] The FN's vice-president, Louis Aliot, agrees: 'Since the 1914–18 war, there have been no more demands for autonomy. The commander-in-chief of the armed forces was called Joffre. He was a Catalan. All sorts of blood was spilt and mingled to achieve, unfortunately through war, the unification of the nation state of France. We want a melting-pot, not a mosaic. The identitarians, on the other hand, are often more for the mosaic and sometimes even for communitarianism.'[27] Too bad for the decentralizing tendencies of identitarian allies and their defence of regional languages—they must submit to the national, statist order of neo-*lepénisme*.

There is something strange about this 'republican turn'. Marine Le Pen projects herself as the only unconditional representative of the will of the people, and if the people wish to exclude migrants, leave the euro or the EU, or discriminate against Muslims, then she will obey their will. Yet at the same time, such is her glorification of the state that it has become the supreme principle—so ultimately, the people are to obey the state. In essence, then, she imagines the people as she would like them to be, since it is first and foremost her own party that wishes to discriminate against foreigners and leave the EU. It might be legitimate for a politician to want a majority of voters to share their ideas; it is less so to pretend that these ideas emerged from the heart of the people in the first place.

The final tactic is cunning, but also a lesson learnt: the choice of apparently consensual historical references that make one wonder to which real French Republic Le Pen is alluding. Needing to refer to a period that will demonstrate the deep-rootededness of the party's ideas in the continuum of national history, she is aware that she cannot look back to the inter-war years, an epoch associated with nationalist activism and fascism. Nor can she refer to the Second World War period—the Vichy state and collaboration with the Nazis; she also refuses to criticize the actions of General de Gaulle, who remains very popular in contemporary French society. Her solution, then, is to celebrate the Third Republic (1870–1940), especially the period from its beginnings up to the First World War. This was the age in which the French Republic was reinforced after a series of monarchical and imperial upheavals, and it was during this time that public education was established.

Le Pen makes the most of general nostalgia for the symbols of the Third Republic's education system—maps of the country's *départements*, wooden classroom benches and pupils in uniform. Against this golden age when *Le Tour de la France par deux enfants*[28] was prescribed reading and the idea of the 'national novel' was celebrated, Le Pen never misses an opportunity to berate what she sees as the Marxist-inspired 'pedagogicalism' that emerged from the ideas of the 1960s. This stands in contrast to the old-fashioned Republican school system, based on effort, merit, respect for the authority of the teacher and the transmission of civic values.[29] Gleefully seizing on the prevailing narrative of a return to authority, she claims that in today's schools,

> the teacher has been turned into an entertainer, if he is lucky enough not to have been reduced to minding a band of savages. The truth is that for more than twenty

> years all ministers of national education ... have on frequent occasion ruined the school system that was once, from the time of Jules Ferry, the pride of France![30]

The theme of secularism also has its source in this period, since the law separating the state and the Church was passed in 1905. Yet this grounding of the new FN's discourse in the early years of the Third Republic goes deeper still. At the end of the nineteenth century, French socialism was consolidating itself and turning towards reformism, while at the same time extolling the notion of the fatherland. This allows Marine Le Pen, with one eye on the working class and wanting to appeal to both right and left, to quote the Socialist figure Jean Jaurès: 'a little dose of internationalism may estrange a man from patriotism, but a strong dose will bring him back.'[31] A large number of the writers she cites belong, at least in part, to this period of history: Victor Hugo,[32] Jules Ferry, Georges Clemenceau, Charles Péguy, Paul Valéry[33] and Georges Bernanos, for instance.

Yet the end of the nineteenth century and the early years of the twentieth also represent an extremely troubled political period. It is true that the Republic was settling down—however, though it was no longer really threatened by monarchists, it nonetheless began to undergo an increasingly severe internal appraisal, which, from crisis to crisis, culminated with the far-right movements of the 1920s and '30s. As the historian Pierre Rosanvallon explains, 'it was at the moment that the principle of the people's sovereignty was no longer contested, and universal suffrage had definitively become the custom, that a new era of reflecting on democracy began.'[34] A critique of the individualism and abstraction inherited from the French Revolution became very widespread as intellectuals sought to construct a more organic democracy, one that would be more than the sum of individual wills, detached from their lived context. The power and the concealed violence of the masses were brought to light,[35] there was interest in the irrational, there was less and less belief in the rule of law and in the virtues of the parliamentary system. It was the age of scandals, such as that surrounding the Panama Canal, which unfolded at the beginning of the 1890s. With Boulangism, the movement created by the populist general and war minister, Georges Boulanger, 'the crisis of the liberal order ... found its expression in the politics of the masses for the first time.'[36] Nationalist sentiment was very strong in a country humiliated by defeat at the hands of Prussia in 1870 and dreaming only of revenge. Thus, Marine Le Pen's references to this period also encompass its virulent and xenophobic nationalism, of which violent anti-Semitism was, from 1880, very much a part. Historian Michel Winock points out that until 1898, when Zola launched his campaign in support of the framed Jewish officer Dreyfus, 'anti-Semitism was viewed by the whole of the left—and particularly by the socialists—as neither a stigma nor a serious threat'.[37]

Certain socialist leaders even considered using the revolutionary potential of popular anti-Semitism.

This historical period, unfamiliar to many in France, is at the origin of a nostalgic republican mythology on which Marine Le Pen plays unreservedly. According to Louis Aliot, it is absurd to 'link the FN to the far right—except if you put Boulanger on the far right. And why not Bonaparte while you're there? And Barrès! Is Barrès a far-right type? For me, he's a republican patriot.'[38] It's all a question of definition, of course, since Maurice Barrès, having developed a xenophobic and anti-Semitic brand of socialism, was one of the great catalysts of a nationalism rooted in 'the soil and the dead'. In any case, the FN's vindication of a 'new Third Republic' conceals a whole series of unresolved issues: popular hatred of elected officials and elites; extreme nationalism, xenophobia and racism; questioning of the rule of law; anti-individualism; and fascination with violence. It is the totality of this 'ideal Republic' that Marine Le Pen would like to resurrect. And yet this was a republic that led to the interwar far-right movements, and ended in Nazi collaboration. Settling for picture postcard nostalgia is a risky business.

6

NEITHER RIGHT NOR LEFT

'When I'm asked whether the division between parties of the right and parties of the left, men of the right and men of the left, still has any meaning, the first thing that occurs to me is that the man who asks such a question is certainly not a man of the left,' joked the philosopher Alain.[1] And we might well disbelieve Marine Le Pen when she declares,

> Let's stop talking about left and right, I think the French are clear about this, more than 80 per cent of them think that there's no difference between the two, and we happen to be with the 80 per cent on that.[2]

What we can say for sure is that wanting to transcend the left-right split that structures political life offers Le Pen every sort of advantage: it allows the FN to escape the far-right ghetto, to stand apart from a 'system' that unites left and right, to gather votes in traditionally left-leaning circles, to reconcile social conservatism with economic anti-liberalism. Even if we can't verify the sincerity of this positioning exercise, we can at least look at whether it is coherent, and to what political currents it is connected. Marine Le Pen has rushed into appropriating the 'neither left nor right' credo, even if it means irritating those in her party who have always defined themselves as on the right, like the ex-number two Bruno Gollnisch,[3] and prompting the emergence of an internal opposition. Marion Maréchal-Le Pen, Marine Le Pen's niece, claims to embody a classically right-wing stance: liberal in economic matters, conservative on questions of values. She is in favour of uniting diverse right-wing tendencies and aspires to be the spokesperson for conservative Catholics (see her anti-abortion positions). Her 'liberal-conservative' faction stands against Florian Philippot's 'national-republicans'. The 'neither left nor right' line, it seems, has yet to prevail definitively within the party.

The extent of the shock caused by the FN's new positioning is evident if, for example, one recalls the presidential campaign of 1974, when Jean-Marie Le Pen, while rejecting a far-right label for his party,[4] fully adopted a right-wing stance on political, economic and international issues. He deplored 'state control of an economy heading implacably towards collectivism' and called for 'the lightening of the state's duties through a progressive restitution of its economic activities to the private sector'.[5] Le Pen was anti-communist, liberal and pro-American, demanding 'a European confederation and France's reintegration into NATO'.[6] Ivan Blot, founding president of the Club de l'horloge (a liberal and technocratic group within the intellectual New Right founded in 1974), explains:

> the right/left conflict shaped political life at that time. The old FN abided by this division through its anti-communism and anti-socialism. Its programme, meanwhile, was close to that of the RPR [the centre-right party of Chirac and Sarkozy]. In the FN leadership, everyone was on the right. That is no longer the case. Another conflict has been grafted onto the original one: a conflict that sets the people against the elites. Now anti-elitism transcends the right/left division.[7]

This fault line began to appear before Marine Le Pen's accession to the party presidency. The FN had achieved good results in working-class communities from the early 1980s, as in Grande-Synthe[8] during the cantonal elections of 1982, where it won 13.3 per cent of the vote. Yet it was not until 1995 that the party clearly articulated the slogan 'neither right nor left, but French', launched by Samuel Maréchal—ex-husband of Marine's sister Yann Le Pen, father of Marion and at that time president of the party's youth movement, though he did not enjoy support across the party leadership.[9]

Marine Le Pen imposed this new line five years later, with the arrival in the party of individuals who came from the left via the sovereigntist-socialist *chevènementisme*, such as Florian Philippot or Bertrand Dutheil de

La Rochère. In her speeches she has not hesitated to reach out directly to those disillusioned with the left:

> As for you, men and women of the left, look what they have done with your hopes. Look what it has become, the left, which was supposed to bring progress, to support the weakest, to defend those who work, who struggle, to bring them a brighter future. It has abandoned all that, betrayed it. Today it has been corrupted to its core by money and by power![10]

In a chapter of her manifesto-oriented book, *Pour que vive la France*, she theorizes this 'organized death of the left', whose origins she locates in the 1970s, namely in 'the combination of the ideas of May '68 with the powerful comeback of liberal economic ideas',[11] that, in the name of emancipation, lead to the destruction of all values and all institutions: 'Nation, Church, Army, School, Family, Traditions'.[12] She concludes: 'For the great and good of the left, it became logical to abandon the defence of French workers, those racist and ignorant rednecks who were about to start voting massively for the Front National—and that was another reason to abandon them.' Thus, in Le Pen's eyes, the left has betrayed itself and is set to disappear, and it is unsurprising that its traditional electorate should turn to the party that claims to defend them best against the impact of globalization: the FN.

The break with ultraliberalism goes back to 1992,[13] when Marine Le Pen began reclaiming a vocabulary drawn from syndicalism, anti-globalism, anti-capitalism and Poujadism.[14] She declares that 'freedom is anything but ultraliberalism', whose 'so-called freedom is that of the fox in the henhouse, the law of the jungle, the law of the strong against the weak'.[15] This discourse is not just directed at workers and small farmers, but equally at all those considered part of the 'ordinary people' (shop-keepers, agricultural workers, craftspeople, factory workers, small business owners, artisans, taxpayers, savers, etc.), or even 'the forgotten'.[16] This last category—she refers in the same speech to 'David against Goliath'—enables her to bring together in a single entity various socio-professional sectors sometimes targeted by the left, sometimes by the right. Refusing to pit workers against bosses, she claims to reconcile their interests around 'social protectionism' or 'social patriotism',[17] in other words her programme of 'national priority'. Her social proclivities therefore rule out any notion of class struggle, as confirmed by Nicolas Bay: 'Marx's analyses are often pertinent, but the solutions are no good, as everything is based on class struggle, which is a complete regression. To set employers and employees against one another is nonsense.'[18]

The other point of intersection between these different sectors of 'the public', previously viewed as divided between left and right, is hatred of the oligarchy. Marine Le Pen paints the portrait of a plucky yet simple-hearted common people, cheated by unscrupulous overlords:

'Trusting, sometimes even naïve, the French have for thirty years handed over the reins of our destiny to men who, under one label or another, have failed in their mission.'[19] She denounces a secret deal between political leaders and economic powers to exploit the French people: 'The frightening increase in misdemeanours and scandals ... demonstrates ... the existence of a veritable pact of corruption that brings together top politicians ... senior public-sector administrators and employees of the CAC 40's big corporations. ... At the same time, this hyper-class uses every trick in the book to take from the little people, the weakest, those who cannot protest or make themselves heard, what little they have left.'[20] This 'Caste in power, whether left or right',[21] she believes, exercises a 'stranglehold on the airwaves by all the friends of power, who monopolize the antennae, who terrorize and censor journalists at press conferences'.[22] The people, then, are to be seen as subject to the power and propaganda of a dominant few.

In her critique of the left's betrayal, Marine Le Pen relies heavily on a philosopher held in high regard in anti-liberal circles, Jean-Claude Michéa, whom she describes as 'hard-hitting'.[23] In a chapter of *Pour que vive la France*, she quotes him with deference on several occasions, referring to 'an illuminating read' but also to 'conversations, passionate debates, which set [her] at odds with certain of [her] friends on such important subjects as secularism, the Republic, free trade, or the end of the euro'.[24] It is thus Michéa, quite involuntarily, of course, who seems to be behind Le Pen's anti-liberal change of direction, and she has asked him to forgive her for 'nationalizing' him.[25] But it is his works, especially *L'Impasse Adam Smith* (The Adam Smith Impasse, 2006), which appear to have helped her to 'theorize the observations made empirically over the years'. In *Les Mystères de la gauche* (Mysteries of the Left),[26] Michéa diagnoses the declining usefulness of the left/right distinction: 'The *denomination of the left*', in particular, is no longer in a position to play a role in the project of rallying 'the people around a programme to abandon capitalism'.[27] He also considers that

> for more than thirty years, the electoral spectacle has essentially been played out against the backdrop of an *exclusive change in power* between a liberal left and a liberal right, which, apart from a few details, are happy to *take turns* in applying the economic programme defined and imposed by the big international capitalist institutions.[28]

Michéa asks himself what this gentrified, middle-class left still has to offer to those disappointed by socialism—but certainly he does not want such political orphans to turn to the far right. For him, their

> attachment to traditional values—from the moment that nobody can be bothered to 'open up' such values, either to develop them in an egalitarian sense or apply them to universal ends—will always be at risk of being

> *instrumentalized* and hence of leading to the most dangerous sorts of political deviation.[29]

But 'we mustn't, in our constant [hunt] for the slightest hint that the "foul beast" [of fascism],[30] has returned, forget that *by definition* these same traditional values stand against the abstract individualism of modern liberalism.'[31] Michéa rejects the far right, but he demands that the socialists adapt to the healthy conservatism of the people—and not the inverse. We can be sure that, if she has read these words, Marine Le Pen has understood which path her party should take: dispelling any suspicions as regards the 'foul beast', in order to draw to her the 'conservative people', victims of mounting inequalities, economic crisis and the failings of the 'cultural left'. In this she seems, at least in part, to have succeeded.

Embracing critiques of the liberal left in the name of the people and a certain attachment to the ideas of Jean-Claude Michéa should not conceal the relationship between Le Pen's 'neither left nor right' slogan and other, earlier initiatives of this sort. Countless politicians now claim to transcend the left/right divide—most recently, President Emmanuel Macron, François Hollande's former economy minister and founder of the La République en marche! movement. Yet if one goes a little further back in the history of political ideas, one will notice that a section of far-right thought has also previously tried this approach. The political scientist Zeev Sternhell has studied this question in particular[32] and, in the case of

France, identifies such a phenomenon—at the centre of the Third Republic. He observes that between 1886 and 1889 the Boulangist movement offered 'the first sutures knitting together nationalism and a certain sort of non-Marxist, anti-Marxist and even post-Marxist socialism'.[33] The Third Republic witnessed the birth of a novel ideological synthesis: the social defence of the people's interests allied to an aggressive brand of nationalism.

The trajectory of one of the period's most famous writers, Maurice Barrès, is illustrative of this movement. At the end of the 1880s, the author who was known as 'the prince of youth' published a fictional three-part series entitled *Le Culte du moi*[34] in which he deplored the melancholy of a young generation that was thirsty for exaltation and disillusioned by the moderation of its political representatives. In 1888 he took the side of General Boulanger, who, recruiting among left and right, attacked parliamentarianism and the bourgeoisie, proposed revenge on Germany for the defeat of 1871, and seemed ready to seize power by force. Barrès became a Boulangist deputy at the age of twenty-seven, claiming to have inherited the Republic and seeking to revitalize it: 'It is simply a case of substituting a true Republic for the hateful despotism of the opportunists. It is a question of having a Republic concerned for the workers' democratic rights, for the unfortunate, in place of this oligarchy of *bourgeois*.'[35] He offered a 'return to the people' in order to 'eliminate the corrupt and the politicians', extolling the 'revolt of the "common people" against the moneyman society organized around the exploitation of France'.[36] This anti-elite populism was strongly tinged with xenophobia, and Barrès called for the protection of French workers against foreign-origin labour. Creating the concept of 'nationalist socialism' in 1898, he rejected class struggle, revolution and the dictatorship of the proletariat, wishing to unite the have-nots and small business owners against immigrants. Opposed to the world of finance, Barrès actively infused his utterances with anti-Semitism, attacking Jewish bankers' and industrialists' supposed grip on the economy.

The combination of left-wing ideas with anti-elite and nationalist right-wing thinking has had various precedents; one of its most notable proponents was the French philosopher Georges Sorel (1847–1922). A graduate of the prestigious École polytechnique and married to a working-class woman, he became—unlike Barrès—a Marxist and a revolutionary. In a 1908 work titled *Réflexions sur la violence* (Reflections on Violence), he offered an anti-democratic and anti-modern view of the left, robustly condemning reformist socialism for its acceptance of the electoral game: 'Today, the parliamentarian Socialists no longer dream of insurrection; if they still sometimes mention it, it is to make them look important; they teach that the ballot paper has replaced the gun.'[37] Disgusted by 'a timid, humanitarian bourgeois class',[38] Sorel eulogized 'the direct and revolutionary method'[39] and, supporting the major CGT trade union,[40] believed that violent conflict would become 'a struggle of the avant-garde'.[41] He added, provocatively: 'I think it would be very useful to give the orators of democracy and the representatives of government a good thrashing, such that none of them maintain any illusions about the nature of violence.'[42] In short, 'proletarian violence, exercised as a pure and simple manifestation of the sentiment of class struggle, seems ... like a very beautiful and very heroic thing.'[43]

Sorel quoted Édouard Drumont—without ever referring to Drumont's self-confessed anti-Semitism—declaring that 'a new feeling has taken possession of the French proletariat: hatred' (Chapter 3, II). Opposed to peaceful democrats and (even this early) to 'human rightists', an apostle of the people's rage and violence against the elites, discreetly anti-Semitic even though he had been pro-Dreyfus[44]—he committed himself to a form of thinking close to the far right, in creating the notion of 'the myth of the general strike'.[45] This characterization of socialism by something other than rationality, by 'an arrangement of images capable of instinctively evoking all the sentiments corresponding to the various expressions of socialism's war against modern society',[46] is typical of the archaic mentality that drives the far right. As a result, from 1910, he moved closer to the nationalist, monarchist and anti-Semitic Action française. Having been the principal author of the anti-modern journal *L'Indépendance*, he was an active participant for several years in the Cercle Proudhon political group.[47] *L'Indépendance*'s introductory statement was unambiguous:

> [democracy] has handed us over to a few big companies of thieves, politicians associated with financiers or dominated by them, who live off the exploitation of those who produce .... It will die from the intellectual revival and establishment of institutions that the French will create, or recreate, for the defence of their freedom and their material and spiritual interests.[48]

This coming together of the far left and the far right would prompt his colleague Georges Valois to remark: 'The intellectual father of fascism was Georges Sorel.'[49]

Italian fascism, which contained a great many other characteristic traits, largely originated in the revolutionary syndicalism of the first two decades of the twentieth century, a movement that turned into national syndicalism and opened the way to fascism.[50] In Germany, certain writers affiliated to the inter-war 'Conservative Revolution' revived the idea of a non-Marxist socialism, as was the case with Ernst Niekisch (1889–1967), who rejected internationalism and advocated national socialism. This 'red-brown' influenced the socialist-leaning wing of the Nazi Party, led by Gregor Strasser (1892–1934), Hitler's unsuccessful rival. Another member of the German Workers' Party and then of the Nazi Party, Gottfried Feder (1883–1941), formulated the Nazis' economic programme in 1920, linking socialism to anti-

Semitism and hatred of foreigners. Among other things, he demanded, chaotically, the banning of citizenship for Jews, the expulsion of non-German immigrants, the nationalization of big businesses, an end to land speculation and the execution of moneylenders. On his arrival in power in 1933, Hitler betrayed the spirit of this national socialism and silenced the demands of the 'second revolution', which was pressing for the implementation of the party's social programme. Even so, the Nazi Party's ideological identity was to remain strongly marked by this mixture of socialism and nationalism.

In France, a similar synthesis was realized by the Parti populaire français led by Jacques Doriot (1898–1945). A Communist Party leader and deputy mayor of Saint-Denis, he founded his new party, with the help of the banker Gabriel Le Roy Ladurie, during the brief Popular Front period (1936–8).[51] Having attempted to bring together the popular forces stemming from communism and the far right, he then threw himself headlong into collaborationism during the war. As for Marcel Déat (1894–1955), originally a member of the Socialist SFIO party,[52] he moved towards fascism during the Occupation and founded the National Popular Rally (Rassemblement national populaire, 1941–4).[53] These two leaders ultimately championed Nazi Germany and its racist and anti-Semitic policies. In other countries, such as Belgium, the solidarist movement, which campaigned for the cooperative cause during the Third Republic, gave birth in the 1930s to a version of the far right that sought to revive the guilds—the pre-modern associations of artisans and merchants. Today in France, Serge Ayoub, former leader of the far-right GUD at the Assas faculty,[54] likes to consider himself the leading light in a movement combining defence of the people's interests with violent ultra-nationalism.[55]

This was the nationalist-revolutionary movement with which Marine Le Pen rubbed shoulders when she herself was an Assas student. The National Front Youth to which she belonged was heavily permeated in the 1990s with a nationalist and anti-capitalist line. Strongly opposed to the United States and to liberalism, the revolutionary nationalists, far removed from the old far right—royalist, Catholic, elitist and anti-popular—exerted a major influence on the thinking of the future FN president.[56] Today, that line has—albeit discreetly—become the party line. It is clearly wrong to claim that Marine Le Pen's FN is similar to Nazi and fascist movements, since manifest differences exist that forbid any such assimilation. But rejecting a *reductio ad Hitlerum* should not conceal the very real affiliation of the 'neither right nor left' credo with an established tradition within far-right European history. In any case, this new political line cannot be considered a definitive exit from the sphere of the radical right. Rather it signals the re-embedding of the FN within another inheritance of the far right: that of nationalist socialism.

7

THE ENEMY WITHIN

For Marine Le Pen, nothing is more sensitive than the subject of immigration, both the most dangerous issue in terms of image and the most vital from the electoral point of view. Ivan Blot considers that rejection of immigration remains the primary and 'real reason why people join the FN, which remains a single-issue party. It is immigration that makes people vote FN. It's perhaps not the most important question for the party leadership, but it is for its electorate. The *basso continuo* of the party is the fight against immigration, a permanent and serious phenomenon. And it is not likely to get any better with terrorism and the migrant crisis.'[1] This preoccupation often goes hand in hand with xenophobic sentiments; attending a few FN meetings and hearing the remarks of those present is enough to confirm this. The FN, moreover, is a movement that needs enemies. Its discourse always presents France as enslaved, invaded, threatened by various aggressors. Marine Le Pen's dilemma is as follows: how, in her declarations, can she project herself as irreproachable and avoid accusations of racism or xenophobia, while at the same time signalling to her xenophobic voters that their feelings against foreigners have her support? Where her father resorted to provocative hinting, she must now make insinuations *without* provoking accusations.

The first move in this strategy has been to remove any suspicions of anti-Semitism. In early 2011, Marine Le Pen stated in the Israeli daily *Haaretz* that her party had always been 'pro-Zionist'.[2] After several statements on her rejection of anti-Semitism and the reality of the Holocaust, and following a failed attempt to visit Israel, she thought that she had finally won this skirmish in 2015, at the cost of a painful break with her father. A year earlier, after his remark about Patrick Bruel (see Chapter 2), she had deplored this 'political mistake', but essentially remained 'convinced that the meaning given to his words stems from a malicious interpretation' before pointing out that 'the Front National condemns in the firmest possible terms all anti-Semitism, whatever its nature'.[3] Refusing to admit that her father had indulged in anti-Semitic references, she thus implicitly accepted his strategy of insinuation, judging it only in political (not moral) terms.

When Le Pen Senior, now honorary FN president, then reaffirmed on BFM TV that the gas chambers were merely a detail of the Second World War, Marine this time acknowledged her 'deep disagreement with Jean-Marie Le Pen, in both substance and form'.[4] Her condemnation was strong: 'The French have been witnesses for several months to an escalation of provocations and personal remarks by Jean-Marie Le Pen that are in complete contradiction with the Front National's political thinking, and with our commitment.'[5] She added that 'I have long-lived and deep disagreements with Jean-Marie Le Pen', without specifying what these were. She would find it difficult to admit that they concerned anti-Semitism, at least, given that she vigorously refuted such accusations against her father in her autobiography.[6] Her reasoning remains above all political: 'Wisdom dictates that one must be responsible for what one says, that one must weigh one's words carefully and above all that one mustn't engage in personal comments', for 'we do not have the right to play with the one source of hope for millions of French people.' In short, everybody can have personal opinions, but nobody can jeopardize the 'de-demonization' of the FN.

This ambiguous message aims to avoid losing the FN's anti-Semitic elements. And though it might seem impossible to pick out the slightest anti-Semitic phrase in Marine Le Pen's declarations, her speeches contain several rhetorical elements of anti-Semitic discourse. This is not the rhetoric of traditional Christian anti-Semitism—that of a deicidal people, responsible before History for the death of Jesus Christ—nor is it that of biological racism, taken up by Nazism. It is rather that of the social racism developed notably by the journalist and polemicist Édouard Drumont during the Third Republic in his *La France juive* (1886), an immense commercial success and the holy book of French anti-Semitism. According to Drumont, Jewish bankers and industrialists had seized economic power and, forming a secret brotherhood, had subjugated, by buying them, both politicians and the press. They were exploiting the people's labour while ruining the country's finances with their speculation, and as strangers to its history, they were seeking global domination by destroying national cultures and traditions.

It's worth looking at this point at the picture that Marine draws of the French political elites in thrall to the world of finance: 'In their arrogance, they thought they could turn their noses up at the slow and laborious construction of our Nation ... in order to create an exclusively virtual world in which their goal would be the coming of a new man, severed from his roots, nomadic, dispensable, a slave to the order of the market.' An exercise in uprooting and separation, she concludes, is underway: France from its long history, the individual from his origins and community in order to subjugate him to a structure that will distort him. This world has been 'dreamt of and theorized by Jacques Attali in his *Brève histoire de l'avenir* (A Short History of the Future), in which he announced with undisguised glee the emergence of (and I quote) "a hyper-empire where hyper-nomads will manage a hydroponic empire". Well, that's what they've done.'[7] Rootless individuals, incidentally of Jewish origin, are thus to be seen as creating a world power in order to exploit the poor and the people—a schema identical to all tenets of social anti-Semitism since the nineteenth century.

Drumont wrote: 'The Semite's dream, indeed his obsession, has constantly been to reduce the Aryan to servitude.'[8] A Jew's aim, he continued, was to 'chase the indigenous people from their homes, from their jobs, a subtle way of stripping them of their possessions first, then of their traditions and customs and finally of their religion.'[9] Marine Le Pen is in agreement in her vision of politicians subjugated by money: 'Each decision taken contributed to this insane objective—dilution of the Nation, weakening of the family, disappearance of national solidarity, negation of our identity and roots, erasing our memory, scorn for values of effort, work, merit, courage, righteousness.'[10] We should recall that, true to a long anti-Semitic tradition, Drumont contrasts the 'enthusiastic, heroic, chivalric, disinterested, open Aryan, trusting to the point of naivety' with the 'mercantile, self-seeking, scheming, subtle and cunning ... Semite'. This opposition of a generous, enthusiastic yet simple-hearted French common people and a manipulative elite reprises a the clichéd image of the elite robbing the people, as we've already seen Marine Le Pen herself express it: 'This hyper-class uses every trick to take away from the little people, from the weakest, from those who cannot make themselves heard or protest, what little they have left.'[11] Thus the new FN's discourse is in line with Drumont and his (more specific) accusations:

> This is what characterizes the conquest: a whole people working for another people that appropriates, through a vast system of financial exploitation, the benefits of others' work. The immense Jewish fortunes, the Jewish mansions are not the fruit of any real work, of any production, but are the foretaste of one race dominating another that is enslaved.[12]

Le Pen concentrates her attacks on a so-called 'cosmopolitan' cultural elite—a traditional circumlocution for 'Jewish'—who, it seems, are intent on destroying the body of the nation:

> I remember very well the declarations of [Bernard-Henri Lévy][13] and Georges-Marc Benamou in *Globe* magazine in 1985: 'Of course, we are resolutely cosmopolitan. Of course, we find everything that is *terroir*, berets, *bourrées*,[14] Breton bagpipes—in short typically French and jingoistic—alien, even hateful. And one of Europe's main merits, in my eyes, is to act as a cooler of such national passion...' It was these men whom Nicolas Sarkozy took on. One, BHL, as a muse, and the other, G.-M. Benamou, in 2007, as cultural counsellor to the president of the Republic! You couldn't make a more symbolic gesture![15]

Another cliché typical of the Third Republic's anti-Semitism lies in identifying the submission of the people's representatives to mysterious powers: 'The candidates of the parties in place are not free men. ... [They] are subservient to pressure groups, to special interest groups.'[16] Of these, one entity above all has attracted anti-Semitic attacks from Drumont onwards: these politicians 'are all subservient to the Bank, having methodically organized the omnipotence of the Bank in the economy'.[17] Today, an anti-Semitic agitator like Alain Soral, a former member of the French Communist Party who has been close to Jean-Marie Le Pen and rubbed shoulders with his daughter, uses the term as a synonym for 'Jewish bank'. In his book *Comprendre l'empire* (Understanding the Empire), he talks of 'the devious victory of the Bank',[18] which frees itself 'progressively from all political power to become itself, in reality, the hidden political power'.[19] According to Marine Le Pen, meanwhile, 'the left ... has surrendered to the bank' and has 'handed over our economy to the tender mercies of the big bankers!'[20] Her language is one of submission and betrayal: Socialist former president François Hollande's friends have 'handed France over to the financial markets!' Here again, Jewish names make an appearance: 'To signal surrender to the financial markets, [Hollande] appointed Pierre Moscovici as campaign director. Now, the French must be told the truth: Pierre Moscovici is the vice-president of the Cercle de l'industrie, founded in 1993 by ... guess who ... Dominique Strauss-Kahn! The Cercle de l'industrie, a pressure group that defends the interests of big business.' In *Pour que vive la France*, Le Pen particularly targets the supposed collusion between business and media circles by mentioning Jewish names: 'Édouard de Rothschild, leading shareholder in *Libération*. And what can be said about Matthieu Pigasse, boss of the Lazard bank and backer of Dominique Strauss-Kahn ...?'[21] She concludes the theme of subjection with an allusion to the Bible:

> They are not free men, they have *submitted themselves to the masters* they have chosen: banks, markets, and then, of course, credit agencies. Look at them all, their eyes fixed on the credit agencies, hanging on their every word as if waiting for the *word of the Messiah*. They are *in the hands of the financial markets, in the hands of the banks*, and perhaps even at the end of their strings, *puppets* in a pathetic little spectacle that is brought back once every five years to make people believe that they oppose each other.[22]

Democracy, she believes, is thus nothing more than a con, a trick produced by the occult forces of world finance.

What conclusion can be drawn from this tight cluster of thematic, lexical and polemical expressions? Perhaps Marine Le Pen is not anti-Semitic, and nor—as far as we can demonstrate—are her utterances, since she never ends up expressing an open allegation of Jewish dominance over the economy, politics or culture. Equally, attacks on finance, on the power of the multinationals, on media consolidation, on the elites' disdain for the people and on their immorality are often formulated by people who have nothing to do with the anti-Semitic tradition. Actors within the world of finance often have very different origins and faiths. And yet it is troubling to see the heiress to a political current that has embraced anti-Semitic ideas several times in its history borrowing the almost entire panoply of anti-Jewish rhetoric. Is she aware of it herself, is it due to her upbringing, or does she simply give speeches written for her by others who sprinkle them with references to social anti-Semitism? We cannot know. But what is evident is that, in her words, the anti-Semitic listener or reader will find what they need to feed their obsession. Accustomed to concealing their opinions, they will be pleased to detect allusions and associations, and will fill in the gaps themselves. The non-anti-Semitic listener, meanwhile, can also subscribe to this discourse, though it's only one step away from turning into socio-economic anti-Semitism. Essentially, it seems that the FN allows a continued subliminal form of anti-Semitism both so as not to lose the support of voters hostile to the bogeyman of Jewish power, and also because its world vision still requires an ambitious, rich, dominant and deceitful enemy 'above'.

But the FN's new, much more clearly delineated target for hostility is Islam—a line imposed by Marine Le

Pen, who sees nothing but profit in it. Her father had an ambiguous relationship with Islam, fighting against immigration while anti-Arab xenophobia thrived during his party presidency, but his pre-independence support for Algerians in France forced him to exercise a degree of moderation. Even today, he recalls, 'As a partisan of French Algeria I was also a supporter of the integration of Algerian Muslims into our country and culture.'[23] His attitude towards Islam, brutal and disrespectful, goes back to his period as an intelligence officer during the Algerian War of Independence (1954–62). He recollects, for instance, the issue of women wearing a headscarf: 'I had reacted: when wives came to see my prisoners, I told them, "No *haïk*![24] Religion or no religion, I don't care!" I said to my prisoners, "If your wife doesn't take it off, you won't see her." And if they protested, I would add: "Of course, others will see your wife. But you'll be able to see the others' wives..." And that worked!'[25]

His position seems to have evolved over several years: 'We mustn't forget that the separation of the sexes in the Muslim world polarizes attention onto what is forbidden. The fact that women are hidden away exacerbates desire. This is where there are profound civilizational differences, and also perhaps incompatibilities, that I might have underestimated,' he observes.[26] His current outlook on Islam stems from a notion of irreconcilable rivalry; he laments a declining European birth rate, the feminization of society, religion's loss of influence, the absence of discipline and the disappearance of any transcendental collective mission—all problems, he believes, unknown in the Muslim world.

> In Africa there has been a considerable advance by Islam ... to the advantage of this religion, since it is simple and normative and does not restrict itself to the spiritual domain, implying sociological and legal forms of commitment. It is underpinned by a dynamism of conquest and even slaughter, and the sword of the Prophet is behind the threat of invasion and submission. Moreover, the word islam means 'surrender'.

He seems to envy such strength, also observing that acceptance of self-sacrifice is less and less apparent in Europe. Thus,

> it is easier for those who believe in paradise and especially for those who delight in the idea of finding young virgins there. The proof is that we are now dealing with enemies who are not afraid of dying. And so what is the only thing we can inflict on them? Suffering perhaps ... When you have an adversary who wishes to die, you don't have many pressure tactics apart from making him suffer while he's still alive. Hush now. Don't make me say what I didn't say.[27]

This organic and natalist conception of geopolitics explains how Jean-Marie Le Pen views Islam as a competitor with the decadent West.

This global and pessimistic vision, typical of a far right that is fond of a pseudo-scientific sort of geopolitics, is not shared by Marine Le Pen. For her, Islam is primarily a political theme that must allow her to convince the French of the validity of her analysis. Implicitly conniving with her father, but also in order to show that she has changed scapegoats, she has taken up the high-risk theme of 'occupation'. Jean-Marie Le Pen had asserted that 'the German occupation had not been particularly inhumane' (*Rivarol*, January 2005). In an echo of this in December 2010, Marine compared Muslim street prayers with an 'occupation'—one without 'tanks' or 'soldiers', but 'an occupation all the same'. She reiterated her remarks on 1 July 2013, likening Muslims to Nazi invaders and presenting herself as leading the resistance. Her father was delighted.[28]

Referring to 'immigration collusion, prayers in the street, halal abattoirs',[29] she also demanded that mosques 'should be modest and not ostentatious with ever taller minarets'[30] and that worshippers should pay for them themselves. In an interview granted to the Turkish newspaper *Zaman France* in April 2013, she insisted: 'The French feel that their ways are under attack. Headscarves, the requirements of places of worship, demands for specific foods ... All that is in contradiction with our culture'.[31] Finally, questioned in the street in March 2014, she stated: 'The FN is not anti-Semitic. ... And today I'll tell you where the anti-Semites are, they are in our neighbourhoods, where they're in the process of jihadi recruitment.'[32] The anti-Semites are the ones that are Other, according to Marine Le Pen, who is tempted to seek the votes of anti-Arab Jews, especially in Sephardic circles.

To justify such a discourse of hostility towards Islam, Le Pen has managed to make several controversial themes her own. The first, which her father never deployed, is the defence of secularism. The 1905 law separating Church and state never prohibited all religious symbols in public places. If that had been the case, points out historian of the Revolution and the Third Republic Mona Ozouf, it would have been necessary to imitate 'our revolutionary ancestors who wanted to demolish church towers in order to bring all buildings into an equality of horizontality [and to remove] from the school calendar all religious holidays. In reality, republican secularism, in the sense given to it by its great founding fathers, only succeeded in establishing itself after a great many compromises.'[33]

Secularization marked the end of the war between the Church and the Republic following reciprocal concessions, but this is not the concept that Marine Le Pen sets out to defend. For her, religious expressions in the public domain, above all if they are Islamic, are to be considered as a violation of secularization. She demands 'secularism for the unity of the nation, through a strict enforcement of the 1905 law: street prayers, which still take place today despite all promises, will immediately come to an end.'[34] Yet, according to the law, this type of religious expression can only be banned in the event of a threat to public order, and as such her proposed enforcement is more akin to a transformation of the law. In the same speech, she added:

> And there will no longer be any question of financing, either directly or in some roundabout way, the building of mosques. The faithful can build mosques for themselves, but with their own money, and certainly not with public money or money from foreign countries that don't respect other religions, especially the Christian religion, as is too often the case! Do they even remember, or perhaps they are ashamed, that France also has its roots in Christianity? Well, that's our history, our tradition, whether they like it or not![35]

The *lepéniste* vision of secularism, then, results in an unequal treatment of religions, for she believes that on the basis of their historical roots, some have more rights than others. Secularism, it follows, must protect Christianity, which is part of French identity, against a more recently implanted religion (Islam). In this respect, she utterly betrays the spirit of the 1905 law in suggesting that secularism is in reality an instrument of Christian France that can be used in defence against a religious invasion. She especially emphasizes that 'Europe is not a caliphate, France is not a caliphate, it never has been and never will be.'[36] In her mind, this twisting of the 1905 legislation in favour of one religion is no contradiction, since she considers that the foundations of the Republic, especially secularism, stem from a secularization of Christian values: 'the principles contained in our national motto "Liberty, equality, fraternity" ... are nothing other than a secularized version of Christian principles.'[37] This somewhat imbalanced brand of secularism boils down to the struggle of Christianity, albeit secularized, against another religion. There is nothing conciliatory about it. Nicolas Bay, the party's young secretary-general with deeply rooted Catholic convictions, confirms this interpretation of things. Secularism 'is a rather Christian concept that requires that we distinguish between the temporal and the spiritual. It reworks the evangelical saying: "Render unto Caesar what is Caesar's, and unto God what is God's."' He has no scruples in acknowledging that Islam is the main target of this Christian secularism:

> The emergence of Islam, which, it has to be said, struggles to distinguish between the temporal and the spiritual, has ended up with secularism again becoming the Republic's defence against communitarianism. Defending secularism is thus a way of showing that we are not only defending our ideas, but above all the Republic.[38]

His conclusion is definitive: 'We want to revive the principle of a Republic that guarantees the equality of rights among its citizens and which allows philosophical and religious freedoms.' And yet: 'For us that doesn't mean putting all religions on an equal footing.'

A second theme, increasingly discussed in French political life and used by Marine Le Pen to prop up her anti-Islamic message, is that of identity. In reality, this term was introduced into the politico-intellectual sphere of the 1980s by the theorists of the Club de l'horloge, the New Right's think tank that brought together senior civil servants. From their perspective, ethnic mixing and cosmopolitanism were viewed as serious risks to European civilization. The theme reappeared in the political domain in 2007 when Nicolas Sarkozy created a 'Ministry of Immigration, Integration, National Identity and Codevelopment'. Many debates ensued concerning the validity of the notion of national identity as well as its explicit link to the issue of immigration. The notion found new prominence in 2013 in Alain Finkielkraut's work, *L'Identité malheureuse* (Troubled Identity). Finkielkraut argues that the rationalist philosophy of the Enlightenment had sought to make the individual independent, to liberate him from all traditional authorities; Romantic thought then reacted against such a movement towards abstraction, and wished to re-root man in real communities and lived collective identities. After the racist disasters of the Second World War, there was a move to abolish nationalism once and for all by constructing a supranational Europe and by glorifying the Other—in particular, the immigrant—even, says Finkielkraut, to the detriment of the host country. This movement would make identity something shameful and 'troubled', or unhappy. Thus Marine Le Pen can, without fear of opprobrium, revive an idea long supported within the FN: arguing that, to defend French identity, Muslims must be stopped from destroying France's so-called traditional way of life.

A third line of attack, which enables Le Pen to defend herself against any allegation of Islamophobia, consists in distinguishing between—but also sometimes confusing—Islam and Islamism. 'We aren't fighting anybody's religion in France. We are fighting Islamist fundamentalism!' she has said.[39] Her argument finds support in the jihadist attacks that have caused bloodshed in Europe and beyond since 2015, and—having condemned 'green fascism' over the past several years—she can even cast herself as a trailblazer in her opposition to terrorists. Here, the entire problem lies in the definition of the term 'Islamism', for Marine Le Pen does not only use it to denote jihadi terrorism, but also puts under the same umbrella traditionalist or fundamentalist Islam, which are not at all the same thing. When she evokes 'green fascism', she is not referring to Al-Qaida or Daesh, but to a supposed stranglehold by fundamentalist Islam on certain urban neighbourhoods. 'These groups have ... taken charge of entire neighbourhoods where they impose their vision, their culture, their proscriptions, their tastes in clothing and food. Headscarves, which until recently were a rare sight, have multiplied, even skyrocketed, in number.'[40] She denounces the 'law of radical Islam' that, she believes,

> prevents girls and women from trying to leave their apartments without wearing a headscarf, that forces those thought to be Muslims to observe Ramadan, that prevents pork being served in dining halls, that insists on halal food, that prevents schoolgirls from doing physical education, that stops men and women enjoying themselves together at public swimming pools, that prevents male doctors treating female patients, that stops young women from refusing to marry men selected for them.[41]

Rather, it is Islamization that she condemns: 'A majority of the French ... are worried about the Islamization of our country, the majority no longer feel at home in France.'[42] The root of the term 'Islamization', however, is not 'Islamism' but 'Islam'. First she conflates the traditional practices of many Muslim countries (observing Ramadan, the prohibition of pork, wearing of the headscarf for married women) with fundamentalist practices (banning any coexistence of men and women, forced marriage); then she claims that such practices are imposed, against their will, on Muslims themselves—and particularly on women—and on others living in these neighbourhoods. In this line of argument, it is well-nigh impossible to distinguish between Islam and Islamism—and that is the desired effect.

Attacks on the 'Islamization' of France give new life to some of the classic themes of the FN and the far right as a whole, such as immigration. One of the most popular slogans at the party's public meetings is 'This is our home', and the idea that Muslims are supposedly seeking to impose their way of life on all, and thus conquer France culturally, is suggested in many of Marine Le Pen's statements. She has had undeniable success here. Moreover, this fear of a France disfigured by the invasive presence of an alien culture is traditional within the far right's political lineage, as seen in a description of Paris by Charles Maurras, the xenophobic and royalist theoretician of the nationalist Action française movement:

> From the first steps that I took in Paris, on the morning of 2 December 1885, I had been struck, moved, almost hurt by the material spectacle of these beautiful streets and grand boulevards adorned from ground floor to roof with a multitude of foreign-looking signs, bearing those names beginning with K, W and Z, which our print workers wittily call the Jewish letters. *Were the French still at home in France?*[43]

Jews in the Third Republic, Muslims in the Fifth—the argument is the same.

Marine Le Pen directly links the issues of immigration and Islamism, drawing on a hyperbolic line of reasoning to conclude that immigration must be reduced massively if future terrorists are to be stopped from growing up in France: 'I commit myself to reducing legal immigration within five years from 200,000 arrivals per year to 10,000, and to limiting very strictly the number of asylum seekers. I commit myself to abolishing the system of citizenship by birth. The acquisition of nationality must no longer be a formality. Naturalization must be subject to strict conditions. Being French is a source of pride, not a right! If the Front National were in power, Mohamed Merah wouldn't have become French.'[44] She has used this argument again since the migrant crisis in 2015: 'Since then, migrants have been wandering around our neighbourhoods, around our railway stations or in shanty towns, leaving France with immense security and public hygiene problems. Since then, terrorism has become commonplace.'[45] The plan to close the borders, at the heart of the FN's project, is thus connected to its new dominant passion: the rejection of Islam.

From year to year, however, Marine Le Pen has shown herself to be increasingly prudent in her declarations concerning Islam. Wanting to break the glass ceiling that she believes prevents her from winning a majority of votes, she offers reassurances to all those repelled by a discourse considered too stigmatizing. But in front of the activists at her rallies, she is less hesitant in pandering to anti-Islamic sentiments. How, then, when each and every word of hers is so carefully examined, does she proceed so as to avoid any controversy or suspicions of a gaffe? To understand this, one really needs to go to her public meetings. At these, in contrast to radio or television appearances, a homogenous whole is on display—an articulate and coherent discourse, but also a total spectacle, where delivery, intonation and suggestion all play a role in the transmission of Le Pen's message.

Stripped down, summarized in a few sentences, this is almost inoffensive—but put back into the context of its subject matter, into a network of allusions and meanings, it is something else altogether.

At her final rally before the 2014 municipal elections, at the Continuing Education Office in the centre of Lille on 20 March, Le Pen didn't even mention the words 'Islam' or 'Islamism'. Four terms were enough for it to be understood what and who she was talking about: 'communitarians', 'fundamentalists', 'school canteens' and 'swimming pools'. These terms act as semantic signals, referring to old allusions to school menu changes aimed at Muslim students, or to adjusted hours at public swimming pools so as to avoid mixed swimming sessions, a red rag frequently waved by the FN. There is no need to be explicit; everybody understands what she means. Such is the semantic strategy of Marine Le Pen's FN, representing the third generation of xenophobic discourse. Before the legal prohibition of hate speech, the far right used to express its hostility towards Jews or Arabs directly. A second generation, that of the FN from 1980 to 2010, had to resort to circumlocution or insinuation in order to convey to voters the persistence of a racist and xenophobic discourse, at the same time as trying to avoid prosecution. Since that time, there has been no point in open complicity, since well-worn phrases are now sufficient to raise controversial issues, letting the listener's imagination do the rest by referring back to older utterances, whether by the daughter or father. The FN has now occupied a prominent place in French politics and media for more than thirty years; its audience has access to a full repertoire of terms that serve as shorthand for previous polemical positions. There is no need to reiterate them explicitly, as *Mariniste* discourse encourages the forming of associations, leaving every individual free to draw, or not, their conclusions. One supporter may make the fundamentalist/Islamist/Muslim connection; another may draw the line at the Islamist.

Some may consider that Islamophobia is less odious than traditional xenophobia: one cannot change the colour of one's skin but one can modify one's religious ideas. Even so, it is worth asking whether attacking a religion is not just as violent as stigmatizing an ethnic group. Religion is either inherited or chosen. In the first instance, it is tied to childhood memories, to faithfulness to a family line, to affection for one's parents. To believe that it is intolerant and pernicious is to denigrate a very powerful emotional and symbolic construct. When chosen, religion is often no less important, indeed perhaps more important, than other convictions and commitments. To devalue or ridicule it amounts to an act of aggression. Marine Le Pen's anti-Islam discourse is highly inflammatory.

Beyond subliminal anti-Semitism and the anti-Islam mood music, non-European immigration is also a target for Marine Le Pen's verbal attacks. She claims not to believe in the 'Great Replacement' theory developed by Renaud Camus—the idea of a plan to 'replace' an indigenous French population with non-European migrants.[46] Yet she sometimes refers to it, gratifying those who do subscribe to the notion. On her accession to the FN presidency, for instance, she spoke of 'a dramatic inverse assimilation' that forces the French 'to live with ways of life or individual or collective forms of behaviour that upset them'.[47] Several weeks later, she was alarmed by 'the exacerbation of extra-European migration' aimed at 'the pure and simple replacement of the French population'.[48] She even referred to a 'veritable secret plan ... of massive immigration and settlement'.[49] In September 2016, she said she feared that France, populated by foreigners, was 'becoming a country that we will no longer recognize, which will have become unfamiliar to us'.[50]

'Big business,' Le Pen maintains, wants to replace the French with immigrants so as to be able to cut pay. Hence the existence of a sort of conspiracy by the economic elites with the complicity of the trade unions: 'I am alone in having uncovered their foul plan to lower wages and introduce generalized competition among French workers.'[51] This idea fits perfectly with the totalitarian schema that she has made the key to her worldview. According to this theory, financial and economic elites—who resemble in every respect the nefarious Jews imagined by Drumont—intend to populate France with migrants, whether Muslims or those from very different cultures. This they would do first of all because, having no roots in the country, these elites would feel no scruples in disfiguring it and in destroying traditional ways of life, and secondly because these immigrants constitute a low-wage labour force. For the cause of strictly economic logic and with disdain for national culture, the elites would sacrifice the people, wrecking France in the process.

The FN's strategy is clear: to avoid any allegations of xenophobia. Marine Le Pen codes her discourse so that it is comprehensible, but unimpugnable. She then systematically links the stigmatization of a race, an ethnic group or a religion to a political problem that can be solved: the stranglehold of economic elites on decision-making, the imposition of a way of life disliked by the majority, or an employer's migrant labour strategy. Yet there is one group of people directly stigmatized by Marine Le Pen: the Roma. To be sure, she does this in her father's rather roundabout way, through a pun, but the intention is to expose this people to general opprobrium—and almost nobody seems to care. In December 2015, at the end of the regional elections, she gave a final campaign speech at the Salle Wagram in Paris. After a favourable first round for her party, she was elated, and electrified her audience. But the moment of communion, when the assembled crowd exploded tumultuously, leaving beside all dry debate in favour of a noisily shared passion, was when she spoke these words: 'The wiping away of redundant political forces is likely to gather impetus when the ultraliberal [Socialist Party] of Valls and Macron joins Juppé's left-leaning UMP [the centre-right Union for a Popular Movement] in a coalition that Mr Dray[52] has already described as 'a rainbow', and for which I found a name several months ago: "the ROM", the Union of Globalist Organizations.'[53] Then came an immense roar, filling the hall.

8

TILTING THE WORLD

Of what sort of world does Marine Le Pen dream? One without globalism, and freed from liberal totalitarianism. In practice, she wants to take part in, even embody, what she perceives as a movement leading to a historic shift. The post-Cold War 'global world'—and, more profoundly, the cosmopolitan and pacified world yearned for by the philosophers of the Enlightenment[1]—must give way to a juxtaposition of identity-based nations. Le Pen wishes to incarnate a France that would place itself at the forefront of this turnaround. Her political adversaries, she says, 'have decreed, as prisoners of their globalist ideology, that history was leading us towards a globalized world without states in which the "American Western model" would universally impose itself. They were mistaken and their error is the starting-point for our decline. From Asia to Latin America, via the Muslim world, a new world is emerging, based on the affirmation of identity and national sovereignty.'[2]

Is this celebration of the West's loss of influence in keeping with French far-right tradition? Seemingly not. We know that Jean-Marie Le Pen adored Ronald Reagan[3] and denounced the Soviet empire—while his daughter swears by Moscow alone. Yet it is not quite so straightforward. A significant section of the post-war French far right was violently opposed to the United States[4] (and to its Israeli 'protégé'). Many such disciples of a 'third way' between capitalism and communism—of solidarism, of the nationalist-revolutionary movement, of 'red-brown' groupings or even of the anti-liberal New Right—have supported Arab dictators, Khomeini's Iran and Gaddafi's Libya, against what they saw as effeminate and decadent Western democracies. Jean-Marie Le Pen would align himself according to circumstance with one or another of their positions; for example, when he disapproved of the American 'Desert Storm' operation against Iraq in 1991. Thus Marine Le Pen's anti-globalization and anti-Americanism—though she does not view Israel as an enemy—are nothing new at all, but a breath of new life into an old far-right motif.

How does she rationalize such a radical view of the world? Firstly, by demolishing the diplomacy conducted by Nicolas Sarkozy and François Hollande. With regards to the former, she attacks 'the systematic alignment of France with the United States, the re-establishment of NATO's integrated command, [the] reorganization of our military presence overseas far from our natural spheres of influence, away from Africa to the Middle East'. Sarkozy, she alleges, surrendered France to the US and waged a disastrous 'humanitarian war' in Libya in 2011. François Hollande, meanwhile, 'reoffended in Syria', because he was 'even more subservient to Obama than Tony Blair once was to George W. Bush.' Condemning the politics of 'submission',[5] she believes that this mindset of alignment with the US corresponds neither to the spirit of France nor to what the country can bring to the world. She criticizes 'military adventures ordered from abroad and outside our borders, our history and our national interests'.[6] Presenting herself as the lone successor to Gaullism, she believes that 'there is something French in the attitude of India, China, Russia, Brazil, Argentina or even Venezuela, in their capacity to say "no" to the powerful when their interests are at stake.'[7] Pressing for the right to diversity in the face of the steamroller of globalism, she takes up the defence of national differences. 'We are marching towards a multi-polar world and we should be delighted,'[8] she asserts, vindicating the 'will to be a power of equilibrium'[9] and not of unilateral subjection.

In support of this symmetry of differences, and the historic realignment that the world is living through, she is violently opposed to all the so-called humanitarian wars waged by the West since the 1990s. 'Democracy,' she insists, 'cannot be exported on the warheads of NATO missiles', for 'democracy is not an export product'.[10] No words are harsh enough to condemn the 2011 intervention in Libya, conducted 'under the putrid influence of Bernard-Henri Lévy, puffed up with his own importance and ever-present when there is a mistake to be made'.[11] She views with the same disapproval the Western impulse to interfere in the 1990s, the American wars waged under the influence of George W. Bush's neo-conservatism in the 2000s and those fought under the banner of 'the duty to protect', as was the case in Libya under the aegis of the United Nations (including Russia and China). Mixing them together, she denounces all forms of this 'unbearable human rights culture',[12] while, liking to think herself pragmatic, she often takes the side of authoritarian or dictatorial states (Venezuela, Iraq, Syria, Libya, China, and so on).

As regards the United States, Marine Le Pen demands an exit 'from NATO's integrated command' 'while remaining a member of the Atlantic alliance', adding: 'We will return to the balanced position that General de Gaulle defined almost fifty years ago and which Nicolas Sarkozy sold off cheaply.'[13] The November 2016 election of Donald Trump to the US presidency delighted her. Her relationship with Israel distances itself from the far right's anti-Semitic and pro-Arab current—represented today, for instance, by Alain Soral. Instead, she has followed the rather more pro-Israeli line of the FN's former number two, Jean-Pierre Stirbois, in the 1980s,[14] or of her ex-diplomatic adviser Aymeric Chauprade.[15] At the same time, she still has to accommodate her 'anti-Zionist', pro-Arab and pro-Iranian networks and friends, such as Frédéric Chatillon, who is close to the Syrian regime.[16] Meanwhile, within the Arab world, she pretends to favour the Shiite axis (Iran-Syria), conveniently aligning her with Moscow's position. Domestically, this also enables her to denounce the alliance between France and Saudi Arabia—'the allegiance [of Nicolas Sarkozy] to the world's promoter of Wahhabism'[17]—as well as the Saudi regime and its links to Qatar. She has long condemned 'those two countries, the rearguard of all the international jihadist movements, [which], through arms and money, fuel terrorism and war not only in Syria, but also in the Sahel, in Afghanistan and even Libya.'[18] Yet Le Pen's stance can be complex and even subject to change, as when she formed ties with the United Arab Emirates in order to solicit financial help for her 2017 presidential campaign.[19]

Her real role model, however, is Vladimir Putin, and she never misses an opportunity to demonstrate her deference toward the Russian president. She 'admires' him,[20] and in this sense offers continuity with her father, who makes no secret of his affinity with Putin.[21] When one thinks about it, one realizes that all the core foreign policies of Marine Le Pen's FN are modelled on those that the Russian president has been developing since the mid-2000s: an increasingly virulent hostility towards the US and NATO, hatred of what are perceived as hypocritical human rights concerns, support for Israel but also for Syria and Iran, an identity-centric, 'rooted' vision of national entities, a desire to unravel the European Union, and so on.

One need only listen to Putin's speech to the UN General Assembly in New York on 28 September 2015 to be persuaded that he and Marine Le Pen share the same vision of the world. According to Putin, it was not good that a 'single centre of domination', 'believing it knows and does better than all others', was born at the end of the Cold War. Dismissing 'American protectorates', he praised diversity: 'We are all different, and this fact must be respected. Nobody is obliged to conform to one model of development.' 'Alas,' he lamented, 'the bloc mentality from the Cold War era and the attempt to seize new geopolitical spaces dominate among certain of our colleagues.' Putin suggested that the colour revolutions (Georgia in 2003, Ukraine in 2004), the Ukrainian Maidan Revolution of 2013–14 and also the Arab Spring uprisings that began in 2011 were no more than American manipulations. He accused the US of causing catastrophes by intervening in Iraq, Libya and Syria, and of having armed terrorist rebel groups. He expressed his belief that in Ukraine 'a military coup d'état was organized from outside'. With feigned indignation, he exclaimed: 'I would like to ask those responsible for this situation: "Are you at least aware of what you have done?"'[22] Speaking to announce the deployment of Russian troops to Syria in support of the president

Bashar al-Assad, Putin was inaugurating a new era of contemporary history, in which anti-Western states, followers of an identity-based vision of international life, would act militarily where they wished in order to defend their interests and their worldview.

Marine Le Pen approves, and formulates exactly the same recriminations—but from a French perspective. Russia supported the Serbs during the Yugoslav conflict, and Putin found it hard to come to terms with NATO's bombing of Serbia in 1999. Le Pen, meanwhile, blames France for 'its participation in the dismantling of Yugoslavia'.[23] While Putin considers the US responsible for the rise in terrorism since the invasion of Iraq in 2003, Le Pen accuses France of impotence in the face of Iraq's breakup, 'now rife with instability, if not chaos'. Where Putin regrets that at the UN Russia did not oppose the intervention in Libya against Gaddafi's forces, she condemns '[France's] active participation in the destabilization of Libya, which has since sunk into anarchy and extreme violence, hence becoming a breeding ground where Daesh can thrive'. Putin fights with brutality on Assad's side against the Syrian rebels; Le Pen mocks 'the [French] willingness, fortunately successfully thwarted, to wage a war in Syria alongside the favourite ally of [our] former foreign affairs minister: the Jabhat al-Nusra, affiliate of Al-Qaida'.

Putin refuses to accept the Maidan Revolution and dismisses it as a 'fascist putsch' carried out by the

Ukrainian far right, while Marine Le Pen denounces '[François Hollande's] alignment with US policy in Ukraine, where a veritable coup d'état was perpetrated against a legal and legitimate government'. She even echoes the Kremlin line on the indissoluble historical link between the two countries: 'Historically, Kiev is the cradle of Russia, a third of Ukrainians are Russian speakers, a large part of the Ukrainian economy is tied to the Russian economy, and so geopolitics cannot be changed.'[24] Logically, she is opposed to Western sanctions against Russia.[25] She concludes that 'France has no global vision', indeed regrets that her country has not adopted a 'Putinian' worldview. Just as Vladimir Putin has launched his 'Eurasian Economic Union', so she—just like her father—supports a 'truly regional and continental politics in Europe, from Brest to Vladivostok',[26] implying the dilution of the EU inside a Eurasia under Russian protection. She would offer Russia 'an advanced strategic alliance, based on an in-depth military- and energy-oriented partnership, rejection of interventionist wars, and support for the international rule of law.'[27] Her dream is of a 'pan-European union of sovereign states including Russia and Switzerland and respecting the status of neutrality, national law and national tax systems'.[28] The FN's secretary-general, Nicolas Bay, likewise has no hesitation in choosing between the US and Russia:

> We support the idea of a multi-polar world to avoid the American model imposing itself everywhere and pro-

> voking war and chaos. We are opposed to the new Cold War that does everything it can to separate Russia from the community of nations. In the Syrian conflict, we can see that Russia is taking a certain number of initiatives that the European nations ought to have taken. This multi-polar world is emerging as a break with the model of American domination that has driven everything for thirty years.'[29]

But Vladimir Putin represents something more in the FN's eyes. Beyond his desire to resist American hegemony, he embodies a political and philosophical model whose principal features the party shares. Since his return to the presidency of the Russian Federation in 2012, he has deployed an overtly anti-Western discourse. Through differing intermediaries,[30] he has initiated an ambitious plan of political influence that seeks to bring together, across the world but particularly in Europe, all followers of a new paradigm. This 'Putin Doctrine' mixes a fierce brand of conservatism (sacrificial patriotism, cult of the leader, appeal to religiosity against a Europe forgetful of its roots and traditions, homophobia) with the exaltation of a specific 'Russian way', which each sphere of civilization may borrow as it sees fit, and with a Eurasian dream on top of this: the project of a power uniting the peoples of Eastern Europe and Central Asia around Moscow—an alternative to Atlanticist might and political Europe. In France, this multifaceted ideology has attracted figures from a diverse range of political backgrounds: men of the left like Jean-Luc Mélenchon or Jean-Pierre Chevènement, leaders from the traditional right like Nicolas Sarkozy, Valéry Giscard d'Estaing or François Fillon—who recycles the Kremlin's line on Ukraine and Syria and aligns himself with Moscow's positions—or right-wing sovereigntists such as Philippe de Villiers, Nicolas Dupont-Aignan—or, first and foremost, Marine Le Pen.

Several motifs here meet with the FN leadesrhip's approval. Firstly, Putinism calls into question the 'spirit of '68', which is accused of undermining notions of family, nation, work, state and authority. In the French context, the polemicist Éric Zemmour, author of *Le Suicide français*,[31] a book that seeks to deconstruct all the values associated with the 1960s, embodies this current of thought. Marine Le Pen holds the same views, adding that the 1968 paradigm consecrated a monstrous union of social protest and hedonistic capitalism. Putin charges 'many Euro-Atlantic countries' with rejecting 'their roots, especially those of Christianity, the foundation of Western civilization', and with abandoning 'ethical principles and traditional identity: national, cultural, religious or even sexual'.[32] A supportive Marine Le Pen remarks: 'Mr Putin is a patriot. He is attached to the sovereignty of his people. He is aware that we are defending common values. These are the values of European civilization,' of 'a Christian heritage'.[33] It might seem paradoxical that Le Pen should flirt with a leader with undisguised disdain for Europe, which he views as decadent. Yet the FN seems to prefer being in Moscow's debt to acting as Washington's 'vassal' and, as such, is clearly affiliated with a country that is gambling on the disintegration of the EU.

Secondly, Vladimir Putin's uncontested dominance in Russia since 2000,[34] at the cost of significant democratic setbacks, panders to French nostalgia for the strongman or providential leader. The cult of personality prevails within the FN, and Marine Le Pen likes to pose as the saviour of a county on the brink of a precipice. During her party presidential campaign, she spelt out her vision of 'the FN's president: they must be like Jean-Marie Le Pen was for forty years, a leader at the head of their troops; they must provide the driving force, be the motor; they must be a general-in-chief.'[35] Thirdly, hostility towards the US brings together all anti-Americans, from sovereigntists to the far left—much to the liking of a leader keen to capture left-wing votes. According to her, 'the voice of France resonates in the world when it doesn't meekly follow the United States—when it cooperates intelligently with all powers, especially Russia, with which we share so many geostrategic interests!'[36] By placing itself at the head of a Eurasian Union launched in 2015 with Belarus, Kazakhstan, Armenia and Kyrgyzstan (but not Ukraine), Putin's Russia intends to counterbalance American power. The fourth motive is Putin's open contempt for political correctness, which he accuses of concealing an unrelenting mentality of domination. Western elites, so the argument goes, are afraid of reality and hence seek to bury it under obfuscation, whereas Putin likes to show that he speaks his mind. Marine Le Pen follows him faithfully in this notion of 'speaking the people's language'.

Finally, fear of the world's increasing uniformity pushes Putin to celebrate national specificities, and Marine Le Pen projects herself as a protector of such diversity, with a mission to defend France against American and globalist influences. She even seems to endorse Putin's statements on the political and moral function of war, telling students in Oxford: 'My generation and your generation have not known war, occupation and barbarism. They have been put to sleep by the gentle music of triumphant globalization, mass consumption, global communication and easy travel, by globalizing culture and King Internet, by individualism.'[37] In short, peace makes people soft, and this is the notion expressed by Putin when he contrasts Russian man, driven by ideals and ready to sacrifice his life, with the pragmatic West, motivated only by material comfort and incapable of risking its existence. With a 'cultural code' but also a 'powerful' 'genetic code', a Russian has nothing to fear from decadent Westerners. It appears, then, that Putin and Le Pen are in agreement with regard to 'the ethical moment in war'.[38]

Marine Le Pen has proudly stated, 'I have never given my allegiance to any power in the world.' This is not entirely true. She follows the path traced by Putin, both officially and very faithfully. She is also financially dependent on Russia.[39] Yet this attitude is somewhat bizarre. Since her arrival at the head of the FN, Le Pen has tried to persuade the public of her party's unqualified adherence to democratic principles, even considering that it is more democratic than all others. And yet the system she takes as her model, in international relations as in politics, generally is not an irreproachable democracy—far from it. The Kremlin—violating the spirit of the Constitution, preventing any other party from taking root, committing electoral fraud, forbidding any real opposition debate and instrumentalizing justice—while always appearing to play the democratic game, has totally emptied it of its substance. And Marine Le Pen does not only defend Putin, but also Bashar al-Assad, as the 'solution' for Syria.[40] The least one can say is that her view of the world is not driven by the ideal of democracy.

Championing a world of differing identities results in a real paradox. As Nicolas Bay explains enthusiastically, 'we are exiting the cycle of globalist ideology and witnessing the return of identities.' Everywhere in the world, from the Hindu nationalist India of Narendra Modi to Recep Tayyip Erdogan's neo-Ottoman Turkey, via Putin's Russia and Xi Jinping's 'Chinese dream', regimes are claiming to represent the religious and/or national aspirations of their citizens. The FN salutes this movement and wishes to glorify the national identity of eternal France. Yet this very return to identity explains in turn the return towards the religious, sometimes mutating into communalism and Islamism—which Marine Le Pen condemns. On the one hand, she welcomes 'identitarianism' in the name of a multi-polar world, yet on the other, she fights against it. The only explanation of this paradox lies in saying that the FN does not defend the Republic against identity politics, but rather one single form of identity politics—French—against another, above all Muslim. By nature, then, its discourse is an ideology of combat.

9

HAS THE FN CHANGED?

Marine Le Pen has imposed a real process of ideological reform on her party. Even if the FN's actual programme has not much changed,[1] she has dropped the anti-Semitic jibes and abandoned the Algerian or collaborationist obsessions of her father. She has anchored the party's discourse in a vision of the world that she claims to be anti-totalitarian. She has done everything to restore its republican references, and she has positioned it as neither to the right nor to the left. But has she, as she maintains, definitively separated the FN from the core of the far right? Marine Le Pen believes that she has swapped a far-right organization for a populist party, and her call to revolt against the elites, the European bureaucracy and liberal capitalism suggests as much.

Against the language of constraints, which for the French typifies the parties of traditional government (the constraints of the EU, of balancing budgets, of conformity to international rules, of concern for financial markets)—and which was embodied by the very liberal programme of the centre-right Les Républicains' 2017 presidential candidate François Fillon—Le Pen appeals for radical change based on a sense of popular discontent. Her proposal for her fellow citizens takes after the Dostoyevskian hero of *Notes from Underground:* 'I say, gentlemen, hadn't we better kick over the whole show and scatter rationalism to the winds, simply to send these logarithms to the devil, and to enable us to live once more at our own sweet foolish will!'[2] If globalization imposed its rules and coercion, and even if it ended up bringing prosperity and harmony, wouldn't we still want to send it packing, if only to prove our independence? This yearning haunts a good many FN voters, and it is worth noting that even while a strong majority of French people are against France abandoning the euro, the party has won increasing numbers of votes,[3] as if rational considerations have not prevented an irrepressible urge to overturn the system. The FN's success promises the intoxicating euphoria of revolt. But is this gesture all that the party offers its voters?

The answer is no. The far right, as we have seen, mixes together four main ideological motifs: the soil, the people, life and myth. Do these still appear in Marine Le Pen's discourse? If so, how? The theme of the soil, the land, is ever-present in her speeches and its rhetoric is very close to the nationalism of Maurice Barrès, who in his 1899 speech *La Terre et les morts* attacked a purely political or administrative conception of France, that of the abstract universalists: 'It seems that in their eyes France has ceased being made up of soil and men to become a theorem, a dialectical object destined to exercise intellectual perspicacity or give meaning to a discussion.'[4] Marine Le Pen takes up the very same idea:

> Oh, I know, France is an Idea, a collection of political principles, a State, a Nation, a Civilization, yes, she is all that, but she is also, above all—and this is all too often forgotten—a land, regions, landscapes, a people of medium or small towns, of villages and fields, yes ... we will always have an ace up our sleeve, the incomparable soil of France![5]

According to Barrès, 'historical precedents and geographical conditions are the two realities that form national consciousness'.[6] Le Pen also sees French identity as determined by its geographical specificity:

> France is most of all incomparable in her geography, her climate, her mountains, her rivers and streams, her fields, her scattered woods and vast forests; she is incomparable in the infinity of her coasts, the extraordinary diversity of her landscapes and the extent of her soils ... incomparable, too, because she simply has the best arable lands, the most fertile soils in the world![7]

Quoting the man of letters Charles Péguy, she eulogizes 'the many crafts of farmers and artisans, from the ploughman to the cabinetmaker, from the wine grower to the potter, of all those "green-fingered gardeners of France"'.[8] Without its land, then, France is nothing. The fruits of this land are not to be polluted by imports from outside: 'from the meats of Auvergne (so long as they don't end up halal...) to the wines of Burgundy (so long as generalized free trade doesn't water them down with wine from Algeria or corks from Transylvania)', products are venerated in 'French cuisine, the crowning glory of so much ancestral skill', if it is not replaced by 'integrated fast-foodism'.[9] This land has to be defended, this heritage preserved, 'this old dough kneaded, worked and made fruitful' against an anti-land anti-people—'those who sneer at our countryside' 'like Bernard-Henry Lévy and his squalid book, *L'Idéologie de la France*, stigmatizing "this incorrigible (and I quote), this incorrigible French people attached to its patch of mud", sic!'[10] Or indeed 'the great league of technocrats who turn the land to desert, who condemn it to lie fallow, who spread the use of Roundup [a pesticide produced by the US company Monsanto] like so much napalm and, finally, exhaust the last small farmers, the artisans, the country dwellers—taking life away from the world's most beautiful lands.'[11] Thus, France's soil faces enemies: cosmopolitan finance and its political or Brussels-based servants. As such, as Barrès put it, 'the land speaks to us and contributes to our national consciousness'.[12]

This defence of the land incorporates an anthropological argument that mixes the theme with that of life:

rootedness. To destroy French soil is to uproot individuals, to transform them into 'a mass of rootless individuals'.[13] Marine Le Pen offers several versions of this theory, whereby a man loses his substance when cut off from his roots. The first of these is intended to be humanistic, and we may recall that she has been known to recruit the philosopher Hannah Arendt (who fled Nazi Germany for France and then the US, where she wrote an article entitled 'We Refugees') to connect rootlessness with loneliness and fragility. 'In our society, where rootlessness is made a principle, everything contributes to leaving individuals isolated in the face of new barbarities,' Le Pen claims.[14] The bond with one's land, in a rural idealization of France, provides a defence against liberalism, which uproots, and Islamism, which deculturates. Lamenting loneliness in rural areas, she wishes to 'make young generations want to remain in the countryside and to return there. This is how we will rebuild links between generations, how we will overcome the tragedies of loneliness and suicide!'[15] Here, her words are a serious distortion of Arendt's thinking, whose concept of rootedness never depended on some rural principle or supposedly pure cultural identity.

This anti-totalitarian reading is, in essence, dependent on a profoundly *barrésien* vision of rootedness.[16] Maurice Barrès was the author of an 1897 novel entitled *Les Déracinés*, in which several high school pupils in Nancy, under the influence of a republican, Kantian and universalist philosophy teacher, leave their native land to try their luck in Paris: 'To uproot these children, to detach them from the soil and community where everything connects them, in order to take them out of their prejudices and into a state of abstract reason, how would that bother him, he who has no soil, no society and, he thinks, no prejudices?'[17] The abstraction of rational thought, Barrès warned, pushes one to 'manage one's life' rather than remaining faithful to 'traditional, local or family habits'.[18] In describing the destiny of these young people, he wanted to denounce the excesses of an empty rationality, detached from the realities of the soil: 'Young Frenchmen are brought up as if one day they will have to do without the fatherland. ... When they are still quite young, their local ties are broken.'[19] Can one really, he asks, make of them 'citizens of humanity, free spirits, initiates of pure reason'?[20] He thinks not, so indispensable is attachment to the soil for a vital and real existence.

A little further on in the novel, Barrès declares: 'In order to allow the consciousness of a country like France to break free, individuals have to be rooted in the soil and among the dead.'[21] This is exactly what Marine Le Pen advocates, in what she sees as a struggle against an even more powerful process of uprooting than that of the Third Republic's republicanism: that of nomadic globalization. For her, rootedness in the land is a precondition of belonging to the French people and of an existence that is not alienated. Such rootedness is natural, as she suggests when stating: 'A tree whose roots are cut one by one will fall: this is what could happen to France if she forgets to be nourished by her own richness!'[22] The Marinist conception of rootedness, therefore, is not based in humanism, but rather in naturalism.

The people forms a central notion in this discursive structure, and it is frequently deployed in order to prove the democratic, republican and socially inclined good faith of the 'new FN'. But this has little to do with the French people as understood in France's republican tradition. Marine Le Pen considers her voters to constitute the people, while those who do not share her ideas are not part of it. Excluded are all who do not share or are not assimilated into her 'traditional' way of life—Catholic, rooted, 'born and bred', settled. And so immigration remains a 'basic problem'[23] because 'the identity of a people, its cohesion, the capacity to get along with one another and to feel united, are really, indisputably, fundamental elements in the life of a nation'.[24] It is for this reason that a struggle must be fought against what Le Pen perceives as 'a migratory tidal wave and advanced disintegration of our national identity'.[25] She concludes, 'The immigration of today is not like that which our country experienced at the beginning of the last century. It isn't true! That's the lie of our age that they want to try to make you swallow!'[26] This affirmation is refuted by various specialists, who stress that current rates of migration are far removed from a 'tsunami' and that, unlike other European countries, France has a very long tradition of receiving foreigners.[27] As François Héran of the French Institute for Demographic Studies (INED) explains, France has undergone

> a sustainable admixture, easier to integrate over the course of time. The 200,000 non-European migrants whom we receive each year add an increase of 0.3 per cent to our population. It's not much, but it has been going on since the nineteenth century. Hence the paradox uncovered by the research of INED and [the National Institute of Statistics and Economic Studies]: a quarter of France's inhabitants are now either immigrants or children of one or two immigrants.[28]

This significant section of the French population is expected by Marine Le Pen to assimilate itself into the mainstream. Such people, having benefited from growing up exposed to a foreign culture, are only conditionally welcome, and she does not count them among those she considers the French people. She also excludes from her definition of 'the people' 'the elites' (politicians, CEOs of big companies, those in the financial sector, journalists in 'the system', left-wing intellectuals) and 'bobos'.[29] These two categories, she believes, despise, subjugate or fight against the people. The population can thus be divided into two parts: the 'rooted' on the one hand and, in opposition, elites, 'bobos' and insufficiently assimilated immigrants—a perspective far removed from the republican understanding of citizenship.

Her definition of the people is based on heritage, for France 'is only eternal through the transmission and glorification of her history. She is only eternal through the toil of men and women who have decided to share a common destiny, with respect for her values and identity: to carry on the millennial work of their ancestors.'[30] Again, this echoes Maurice Barrès: 'We are the product of a collectivity that speaks inside us'.[31] Such a process of transmission, according to Le Pen, has taken place in part 'through the enchantment of our landscapes and the spiritual strength of our churches'.[32] Those who do not recognize themselves in those enchanted landscapes, in the 'spiritual strength' of Catholicism, in these 'traditions' or in the 'examples of [France's] heroes who have inspired the dreams of entire generations of French youth', are not, in fact, 'heirs to a great people'.[33] They are automatically excluded, and must then demonstrate that they can join the people. Moreover, she says, 'the amnesiac elites ... are tired of this heritage and never stop defiling, weakening and dismembering it'.[34] To illustrate her line of thought, she quotes François-René de Chateaubriand:

> Religion and morality are subverted; the experience and customs of our fathers are disregarded; the tombs of our ancestors, the only solid basis of all governments, are destroyed—all to form, according to the dictates of a fallible reason, a society equally careless of the past and the future. Blundering in our own follies, having lost all sense of justice and injustice, of good and evil.[35]

Without reverence for a French past transmitted by ancestors and culture, there can be no people, and it is in this context that the family is emphasised as the final line of defence against the negation of historic roots. If the state and the school system no longer carry out this vital task, then the family, a protective sanctuary from the abstract coldness of the state, enables 'the perpetuation of our fundamentals, the transmission of our knowledge, the conservation of our formidable cultural patrimony, the defence of our identity'.[36] As such, family is 'the central and fundamental pillar of society'[37] and must be considered 'sacred'.[38]

For Le Pen, a people like this, formed by a shared heritage, must ultimately recognize the existence of a collective spiritual principle, which she calls the 'national soul'. Speaking in front of Joan of Arc's statue in Paris in 2011, she exalted 'the soul of our people', built by the French through 'the links of a chain that ties us to the past through our history and to the future through our will to achieve our destiny'.[39] The celebration of a collective soul, a traditional theme in nationalism, allows Le Pen to break the vicious circle of abstract individualism whereby one citizen is the equal of another: 'A people is not simply the sum total of individuals ... just as the Nation is not the sum of individual histories or sectoral interests,' she insists, underlining her anti-materialist and anti-judicial credo: 'A people and a Nation are also the conjunction of immaterial realities: the tenderness of family, love of landscape, consciousness of the history that forged them, the spirit of collective service and sacrifice, the communion of values.'[40] 'The soul of France lives in each of us,' she repeated in 2015,[41] laying out her spiritualist and essentialist conception of the French people.

Yet she also believes that the people must be disciplined by a superior order, that of the state, since 'without order a society cannot be free'.[42] In support of her view she again quotes Charles Péguy, who 'was infinitely correct when he declared that "order, and order alone, definitively makes liberty. Disorder makes servitude."'[43] This order, moreover, has been guaranteed by a spiritual and religious principle: that of Christianity: 'Pacification, social harmony and collective feeling only returned [after the fall of the Carolingian Empire] thanks to religion, Christianity and its secular Capetian arm.'[44] Protestantism, by contrast, is viewed as a factor of discord: 'With the Reformation, that is to say the Protestant schism that was the first manifestation of individualism, unity could no longer be built around Catholicism.'[45] This looks back to the anti-Protestant obsession of a thinker like the monarchist Charles Maurras.

The combination of themes of identity through heritage, the soul of a people, and order and the role of Catholicism further shrinks the parameters of Marine Le Pen's definition of 'the people'. Informed by an anti-Enlightenment strain of thought, her vision of the people in any case has little in common with its republican definition. Her 'people' may not be a racial or ethnic construct, but excluded from it are all those who do not claim to be at least cultural heirs to this idealized vison of 'eternal France'.

As we saw in the introduction, the theme of life is fundamental to the far-right tradition. Against the reign of the rule of law born out of republican norms, some late nineteenth-century writers posited the irresistible power of life and popular instinct. This was primarily a vital principle deaf to rationality and symptomatic of attachment to the land; then there was another motivating force, survival, which fuelled revolt against oppression. The former principle is, once again, drawn from a reading of Maurice Barrès, but the theme runs through the entire history of the far right. One of the novelist's favourite words is 'carnal',[46] and carnal attachment is the preserve of France's 'real' children, ready to protect her come what may—and hence excluding, yet again, recent arrivals and all those who are 'rootless'. Such love is inexplicable and passionate—herein lie its strength and beauty—and Marine Le Pen on several occasions has reworked this far-right fetishistic term, claiming that 'this carnal fatherland ... is inscribed in every one of us'.[47] She has also evoked 'the [existing] physical bond between the French people and its army, just as there is a physical bond between the French people and France'.[48] Thus the physical, or carnal, connection to the nation supersedes the election of the people's representatives and the pre-eminence of the rule of law.

Marine Le Pen does not view historical and political life through the category of concepts and expressions that are open to the rational, but rather through attitudes and reactions based on notions of life and the physical realm. To favour the corporeal or tangible over the abstract is the very basis of the far right's tradition, and this systematic position underpins Le Pen's entire discourse. This is even more striking when one attends a meeting or rally, where her physical presence and passionate rhetoric are intended to weld the audience's collective body and give those present a sense of invincibility. With fervour and fury, words become physical, allowing the audience to grasp the truth of what, according to Marine Le Pen, is happening in France. This reality is one of submission 'to our new masters',[49] the globalized elites. Such servitude is voluntary and accommodating: 'We no longer have control over our sovereignty since the entirety of legislative procedure consists of a servile rewriting of EU directives; the sheep in parliamentary flock only have to follow the tracks that their new master might deign to show them.'[50] In a lexicon of humiliation, France's elected officials are not, she maintains, leaders, but, on the contrary, the slaves of foreign or supranational powers. 'You, the president of the Republic, ... you are indeed a "normal president"[51] because for thirty years normality has amounted to taking orders from Berlin, Washington or Goldman Sachs.'[52] When not treated as subjugated slaves, those in power are seen as reproachable children:

> Our ministers are no longer anything other than pupils with more or less good marks in the "European senior form", Frankfurt's darlings, Brussels' dunces or teacher's pets ... This humiliating metaphor of the classroom ... has become a reflection of reality. Our rulers infantilize the people because they themselves are infantilized by the masters they have chosen and imposed on us against our will.[53]

Nothing is spared in Le Pen's efforts to instill in her audience an irrepressible feeling of physical discomfort, shame and anger.

The body becomes the ultimate metaphor, but not any body: one that is humiliated, belittled, mocked, even violated. While political leaders 'have chosen to bow their heads to the forces of money', 'the French people had decided to lift theirs up, to hold them high'.[54] The symbolism of lowered head and eyes and bowed back comes up frequently: 'we must draw from the depths of French consciousness ... the capacity never to bow down before the powerful';[55] 'I ask of you, Frenchwomen, Frenchmen, never give up! Never lower your gaze! Never bow down!'[56] Such submission is all the more degrading when it is to humans described as animals: 'Let's stop flinching in front of these illegitimate masters, these parrots.'[57] The political class is animalized: they are 'the packhorses of the system, the old wolves of politics that they try to palm us off with so that they can sell us their old and out-of-date junk once again.'[58] Nicolas Sarkozy is labelled 'an old warhorse'[59] and a 'creek crocodile'.[60] Animal insults, it should be recalled, are a favoured turn of phrase in Stalinist or fascist rhetoric.

Le Pen also evokes the physical manifestations of fear: 'There is no reason to tremble because we can take back control.'[61] Yet the strongest image remains that of prostration, the apotheosis of humiliation, and she rails indignantly against 'that power which lies down before Finance',[62] against political leaders 'always ready to bow and scrape',[63] or against Nicolas Sarkozy 'ready once again to lie down in front of the injunctions of an unelected European commissioner'.[64] Revolted by the idea that the former president might '[show] his muscles', it is more a case of 'hard words and soft hands',[65] and she rejoices that he received, in her view, 'a monstrous slap in the face'[66] in the 2015 regional elections. As for François Hollande, she attacks his 'puffed out chest' and 'weak arms'.[67]

The final life-themed tactic used by Marine Le Pen to incite hatred and anger her audience is the imagery of violence, sometimes coupled with sexual connotations. She hints at the intolerable prospect of girls abused and young men martyred by thugs: 'How can one love France when one allows her sons and daughters to be brutalized by an ever more radical violence, by an ever more savage delinquency that is killing our children?'[68] The vocabulary of prostitution is also deployed to induce disgust: France is characterized as 'the mistress of the United States' and 'the harlot of paunchy emirs'.[69] Some metaphors come close to being obscene: 'The old ladies of our electoral campaigns tart themselves up a few months before the election as frisky young girls in the hope of enticing the French people once again. But behind the powder are the wrinkles, behind the seductive poses is a political and moral fraud.'[70] Terms alluding to greed and gluttony proliferate: 'the big beasts of finance' have a 'voracious appetite' that can only be satisfied to the detriment of 'the decent people',[71] and it is the state that keeps the financial markets 'fattened up'.[72] Finally, her language approaches insult when she castigates, for instance, 'all those phoney candidates or ... all these hucksters of French political life'.[73]

Against all such physical humiliation, Le Pen endorses 'the vital instinct of a people',[74] a notion that calls to mind her father's survivalism. A natural impulse of this type is indeed defined by 'a survival instinct'[75] among 'a patriotic generation, who have understood everything, and who have no intention of being crushed by a vile world order where they have no place'.[76] The instinct in question transforms itself into a popular eruption of feeling against the masters (politicians) who have become the slaves of the real masters (financial elites). This reaction, according to the traditional exaltation of violence by the far right, should be seen as healthy: 'Let us march side by side and strike together.'[77] The time has come, says Le Pen, to fight: 'It is war, my dear compatriots; yes, it is war: the globalist enemy has won many too many battles.'[78] With a discourse exhibiting many of the life-exalting and bellicose aspects found in far-right thought, Marine Le Pen's aim is to whip up anger, even if it means opening the door to violence. Here again, she is a long way from her slogan 'France at peace'; what emerges from her speeches is rather 'France at war'.

The final cornerstone of the far right's ideology consists of myth, and Marine Le Pen has developed a suitably mythical vision of France's history. Eternal France once knew a golden age, but it has been ruined. Yet the country will find salvation, thanks to a heroine, a new Joan of Arc.[79] This attitude is a response to the desire to idealize and essentialize the political, but other mythological elements found in Le Pen's thinking are more specific to the far right, albeit more discreetly than in her father's discourse. The myth of decadence, for instance, appears in her speeches, even if she avoids the term itself.[80] She regularly depicts

> that miserable form of inertia and decrepitude that everyone feels when they think of our country ... that terrible feeling that nothing can any longer remove it from the long and painful path towards annihilation. This is what provokes in us such a horrible thought: that the end of France is now more likely than its recovery.[81]

The downward trajectory seems inescapable, she continues, for 'nothing changes and each day the country sinks a little further into the feeling of an inexorable decline, of weakening influence, of regression, of a descent into hell.'[82] The peril is existential since 'this abyss ... is one of ruin, invasion, enslavement and extinction as a people and nation'.[83] Alluding to historical analysis of the decadence of the Roman Empire and its disintegration and destruction, Le Pen uses the term 'barbarian'. Firstly, 'There is much more to French youth than the hordes of barbarians who pollute our high-rise suburbs.'[84] As in the late Roman Empire, the onslaught is both internal and external: 'It is ultraviolence, sometimes barbarity, raging and spreading, sparing almost nowhere, affecting most the poorest and weakest among us.'[85] In this allusive fashion, she systematically makes the link between immigration, Islam and delinquency.

Ultimately, Le Pen does not share a cyclical vision of history, and she promotes a vision presented in terms of progress for the French. Yet her discourse remains strongly pervaded by this myth, very fashionable among the pagan far right. She refers to 'the end of a cycle' that began in the 1960s, with its ideals of common ownership and welcoming foreigners—and which led, in her view, to permissiveness, the weakening of patriotic sentiment, historical amnesia, the reign of the politically correct, intercultural tendencies, Islamist terrorism and narrow vision. She is convinced that throughout the world, from Putin's Russia to Brexit Britain, via Trump's America, Orbán's Hungary, Poland, Austria, China and India, an 'identitarian' cycle is starting to emerge. This movement, according to her, is inevitable: 'Historical cycles cannot be stopped.'[86]

Her terminology is also very often linked to a form of cosmic symbolism. 'France, and with her all the French, is in the dark of night',[87] she has stated, before rejoicing that 'the sun of renewal is rising'.[88] Referring to the presidencies of Nicolas Sarkozy (2007–12) and François Hollande (2012–17), she views their time in power as 'always the same tunnel. That long and dark tunnel that descends into hell.'[89] However, 'In these dark times, in France's night, now is the moment to shine a light for the French. ... It is the light of hope. It is the light of rebirth of the Nation and of the French people.'[90] And who might embody this new dawn? Modestly, Le Pen admits: 'Nothing in reality predestined me to be here before you, chosen to take the lead in the great battle for the renewal of our country.'[91] The vision is both sublime and cosmic.

Finally, although Le Pen refuses to identify with the many conspiracy theorists who today populate the far right's digital realm, her worldview points to several levels of obedience or allegiance to higher powers that are difficult to define. Conspiratorial at heart,[92] she sees herself as alone in revealing to the French the real hierarchies that govern the political and social life of their country. She insists that this truth is emerging little by little, as is evidenced by her growing following: 'Today, when exasperation is gaining ground, when above all *the veil is torn away* and by our hand, the hour of real change can strike.'[93] Marine Le Pen's self-image is as the agent of an awakening, who will expose the truth concealed by the media, themselves subjugated. Her view is entirely coloured by the myths of decadence and salvation, of conspiracy and rebirth. And here, once again, we recognize in her discourse the four founding pillars of the far right's ideology.

CONCLUSION

The new Front National's discourse is ultra-securitized and unassailable. More than anything, Marine Le Pen wishes to avoid falling prey to a 'word too far'—like the Holocaust 'detail' that left a mark in many minds and prevented her father from winning the votes of a majority of citizens. While supporting a programme that is overtly opposed to immigration and stigmatizing Islam, she is careful never to 'go off message'. Euphemisms, implicit epithets and code words allow her to avoid being charged with open xenophobia. In order to attack Islam, she talks of defending secularism and feminism, refers to communalism and throws in shorthand references (school canteens, swimming pools, halal abattoirs, mosques, Islamism). She wraps this phenomenon she won't name in a lexical net that fails to deceive many, but which permits her to evade accusations. Le Pen moves behind a mask, and she is very good at the game. In order to give the impression that she has left the far-right family, she has left multiple false trails, covered her tracks. Ultimately, she has distanced herself from all those who could compromise her quest for respectability, including her own father. This is how she intends to achieve supreme power.

Marine Le Pen does not only show skill in her handling of language. She has also developed a seductive view of the world that is both dizzying and profoundly felt by many people. She offers the dual pleasure of a comprehensive explanation and a sensitive recognition of her audience's concerns, responding to feelings that are hard to define, indeterminate worries and intuitions that she frames with real talent. In short, she provides a key for understanding reality, and another for transforming it. This is the strength of her ideology, and on a foundation as coherent as this she believes she will eventually win the support of the majority of citizens.

Yet what does she have to say, apart from truncated quotations from authors who are often grossly misappropriated? That a form of invisible totalitarianism has placed its leaden weight on the country. It has been put there by 'globalized elites', in other words those who have symbolically left the national soil in order to pledge allegiance to the liberal economy, and above all the world of finance. The anti-Semitism born at the end of the nineteenth century designated these 'masters' as Jews. Marine Le Pen has abandoned any such accusation, but she has retained the full conceptual apparatus linked to this brand of economic and social anti-Semitism. Anybody can interpret this presentation from an anti-Semitic perspective, but nobody is forced to. She adds that these masters have succeeded in making their domination more or less bearable—which only increases its perversity—whereas in reality, they have created a liberal, consumerist and pro-immigration ideology. Echoed by the media, they brainwash ordinary people by making them believe that happiness lies in consumption and that success lies in resembling the masters themselves. But, essentially, they despise the common people who have—so far, at least—maintained their traditional virtues. The world of Marine Le Pen is somewhere between George Orwell and Michel Houellebecq.

And so she calls for anger, and for a popular insurgency against the masters of the world and those whom they have arranged to 'replace' the true French: immigrants from outside Europe, Roma and, above all, Muslims. She encourages a movement against the traditional parties and their globalized 'godfathers', against the bourgeoisie and the bobos, against immigrants and Muslims, against the debilitating 'spirit of '68', and in doing so she asks for the support of the ideological leader of 'identitarian' Europe, Vladimir Putin—support that he is more than willing to provide.

Marine Le Pen has undeniably transformed her party. She has replaced her father's pseudo-scientific discourse with an alternative vision that has clear political consequences: the claim to republicanism, the rejection of the right/left divide, the shifting of xenophobia onto Islam.

Yet she has not demolished the traditional pillars of the far right; she has simply brought them up to date. She has not knocked down the far-right walls to build a new home; she has only moved the furniture around. Far from renouncing the far right, she has brewed it anew, with fresh ingredients. The strange republicanism of Marine Le Pen excludes a section of the population in favour of those of French stock, and this is part of a wider theory of cultural rootedness. Her positioning of the FN as 'neither right nor left' resurrects one of the most important parts of the far right's outlook: national socialism. Instead of looking to an old ideology, conservative but open to capitalism, she has brought back into fashion the dream of a third way, just as opposed to liberalism as to everything foreign or anti-popular. We must realize that her reconstruction of a worldview, drawing on new writers and discreetly recycling old ones, has made far-right thinking more solid and ambitious than before. Marine Le Pen has not eliminated the far right in the slightest. She has given it new strength.

EPILOGUE TO THE ENGLISH EDITION

17 April 2017. Far from the rustic, fête-like ambiance of the public meeting in Brachay that opened her campaign seven months ago, the atmosphere at Marine Le Pen's last big rally before the presidential election is feverish. In the passage leading to the Zénith Paris arena, a young man leans toward an older couple and jeers, 'Fascist pigs.' Without even turning round, the husband throws back, 'Faggot.' Meanwhile, far-left counter-protesters are disrupting the event. Molotov cocktails are thrown at media-friendly lawyer and Marinist disciple Gilbert Collard as he gets out of his car.

The rally begins. In the stands, groups of friends unfurl their banners and Tricolour flags. Marine Le Pen, her loud voice tinged with fatigue, contrasts true 'patriots' with those who are 'after her', and who want to 'sink [France] into the vast lava of uncontrolled globalization'. She offers a 'fraternal vision of union among the French people—a union built around our bloodlines, our intangible heritage, our traditions, our beautiful language, our culture, our way of life, our understanding of the world and of mankind, our values.' When she mentions her rival candidates, the audience responds by shouting insults, chanting, 'This is our home!' Le Pen takes up the mantra: 'This is our home. And that means that we've had enough of a France where the law of the Republic no longer rules, enough of housing estates where local bosses enforce the law of gangs, drugs and mafias'.

When she declares, leaning on each phrase, 'that in France we respect women, we don't harass them in the street with coarse and offensive language, we don't bar them from public spaces, we don't beat them, we don't ask them to hide themselves behind veils because they're supposedly impure', a girl appears on stage with a bouquet of flowers, throwing them over Le Pen and attempting to bear her breasts. The security guards descend on her and roughly throw her out. The murmur goes round: she's Femen![1] Unperturbed, Le Pen calmly resumes her speech. She lays out her plan for closing France's borders, with an immediate moratorium on legal immigration. This is new. With just a few days left before the first round of the election, Le Pen is nervous, looking to consolidate her voter base around one of its timeless obsessions: immigration.

Her campaign is running out of steam. After months of feeling confident that she would make the second round, now Le Pen is worried by the rise of Jean-Luc Mélenchon, the 'left-of-left' candidate for La France Insoumise (France Unbowed), who is stepping on her toes with his anti-elite rhetoric. In her pursuit of international recognition, she has sought but not gained the support of Donald Trump, with whom she didn't get a meeting during her trip to New York in January. On 24 March, on the other hand, Vladimir Putin received her in Moscow. The Russian president, who has become the subject of heated debate among the French presidential candidates, fears a victory for Emmanuel Macron, who certainly doesn't represent the conservative revolution that Putin wishes to impose across Europe. But during the first-round election debate, Marine Le Pen hardly gives a brilliant performance. Now, having spent months sugar-coating her rhetoric, she even fears being shunned by her own electorate if they are tired of this 'detoxification', which some view as trivialisation, if not betrayal.

* * *

The results of the first round on 23 April are disappointing. Yes, Le Pen will be on the final ballot, following in the footsteps of her father's 2002 campaign. But with 21.3 per cent of the vote, she is significantly off the 30 per cent she'd hoped for. Short of a miracle, she has very little chance of becoming president. She now stakes everything on an alliance with the sovereigntist right-wing candidate Nicolas Dupont-Aignan (Debout la France), who received 4.7 per cent of the vote. This alignment will cost her dearly: she has named Dupont-Aignan as her future prime minister, which has the FN gritting its teeth; she has also given up several key elements of her manifesto, making her look capricious and spineless.

In particular, she has announced that moving from the single currency to a common currency—that is, leaving the euro—'is no longer non-negotiable'. This shift will prove fatal. In the big televised debate between the two rounds of voting, her opponent Macron backs her into a corner on this defining feature of her manifesto. Her pronouncements are vague, she scribbles notes throughout and can't seem to get her papers in order. Her plans to reintroduce the franc, or even adopt a dual currency, alarm part of the electorate, particularly the older demographic. Sitting opposite Macron—a young, moderate, firmly spoken and well-informed technocrat—she comes off as an incompetent fanatic. Even her own team are dismayed. Questions are starting to be asked about what actually separates her from her father, who put invective and provocation ahead of the desire to gain power. What if Marine Le Pen, too, is secretly afraid of being in charge, and would rather remain a doomsday prophet on the sidelines?

* * *

As expected, Marine Le Pen lost the second round on 7 May. With 33.9 per cent of the vote, she found herself well short of the vote share she had aimed for. The fallout somewhat resembled a descent into hell. Deflated and exhausted, she then had to face her young and popular niece, Marion Maréchal-Le Pen, announcing her temporary withdrawal from politics. The outgoing parliamentary deputy, leading champion of the 'liberal-conservative' hard line, is taking a step back, waiting for the opportune moment to come back stronger—and, perhaps, take over the party leadership. Meanwhile, Florian Philippot, Marine's most loyal adviser and the hand behind the new 'national-republican' party line (anti-EU, socially-minded and secularistic), has found himself under brutal attack by colleagues. His response has been to start his own branch of the party, The Patriots. He has even threatened to leave the FN if the policy of leaving the Eurozone is revisited. Discord is rife at the very heart of the party, and completely drowned out its campaign for the June parliamentary elections.

The demobilization of the FN electorate was evident at the polls. In the first round, held on 12 June, 55 per cent of those who had voted Le Pen in the presidential election a month earlier abstained.[2] Eight FN candidates won seats in the end, including Le Pen herself, but that isn't enough to form a parliamentary group, which requires at least fifteen deputies. The FN has failed to become the parliamentary opposition (against Macron's majority), and in the first debates of the new session its MPs were conspicuous by their absence. When they did show up, they laughed off their own amateurishness.

Le Pen's priority now is to save her own skin as party leader. She has promised that 'everything will be different', even the party's name. She declared her intention to bring together a broad coalition involving other movements and well-known political figures—but by the end of the internal party seminar held on 21–22 July, only one question had been more or less settled: the fate of the euro. New FN policy is that France's exit from the single currency can wait until the end of the current parliamentary term in 2022. It's no longer a priority. Futhermore, Brexit has lost its status as the model for a future Frexit. At the time of writing, the next party congress (due to be held in February or March 2018) is expected to further outline the FN's reconstruction, following a 'big consultation' scheduled for autumn 2017. The key decision is whether the FN should continue its 'neither right nor left' strategy—which has been the secret of its recent successes, notably in Northern France, and which, despite defeat, has allowed the party to become a major political force—or whether it must now submit and return to the fold of the right, as one party among others within France's conservative movement.

And so, once again, the party must undergo a self-imposed revision of its ideology. We've had the father's FN, defending white Europe against African or Asian 'invaders'; we've had the daughter's FN, defending France's little people against the globalization conspiracy and its Islamist allies. Are we now going to see a third FN, one that has shaken off its far-right references but remains identity-focused and conservative, in alliance with the right wing of the mainstream Les Républicains? Whatever the ultimate form of this promised rebuilding, one question will remain: why did the powerful momentum built by Marine Le Pen fail to bring victory in the 2017 electoral cycle? For many commentators, the turning point was her defeat in the televised debate against Macron. For them, at that critical moment, Le Pen showed her true colours: as a woman who revels in hateful attacks on others, but isn't equal to assuming the demeanour of a head of state.

All this is true, but it's not an adequate explanation. This televised moment of truth wasn't just a mishap in an otherwise flawless campaign, nor even a break from an earlier project of seduction. It was simply a logical inevitability. Marine Le Pen's 'de-demonization' of the FN has been anything but a liberalization of her father's radical discourse. She has simply replaced one far-right ideology with another. It makes perfect sense that her performance seemed just as detached from reality as her father's. Detoxification may have won the FN votes. But it has also locked the party, to an unprecedented degree, in a way of engaging with the world that is purely ideological. For years now, Le Pen has been hammering home a discourse against 'globalized elites', guilty of a vast conspiracy against the people. She has proven that it is both clever and effective, allowing her to engage with a wide variety of policy areas and seduce new anti-liberal voters from both right and left. But, in the end, she has also trapped herself in this ideology. At rally after rally, she explained to her audience that the world they live in is a totalitarian system; that behind the façade of freedom they are ruled by a ruthless dictatorship, a thought police that controls and stifles their way of life. She outlined a paranoid vision of the world, where politicians and journalists are all shameless liars, and offered only one single explanation for all of today's issues: a globalist-Islamist alliance, remote-controlled from the world's financial districts. She appealed to the bleaker passions of her fellow citizens: fear, hate, the desire for revenge, or even for violence.

She convinced a third of French voters, which was a huge achievement. But the majority still believe that the world we live in is complex; that there isn't one single cause behind all its problems; that the idea of living under a *Truman Show*-esque totalitarian yoke might be strangely thrilling, but is far from the reality; that positive messaging works better in politics than naysaying. Ultimately, the electorate chose not to fall in with Marine Le Pen and her depressing, conspiratorialist discourse. Not this time, at least—for there is no guarantee against such rhetoric making even further gains in the years to come, particularly if Emmanuel Macron proves to be a disappointment. While this sort of ideology goes unanalysed, and is not understood, dissected and refuted by its opponents, it will always be a threat to French democracy. The demon has not yet breathed its last.

Paris, August 2017

NOTES

INTRODUCTION

1. A reference to Jean-Marie Le Pen's refusal to condemn the *Charlie Hebdo* terrorist attack in January 2015, when (in response to the widespread solidarity slogan *Je suis Charlie*) he remarked that he was not Charlie Hebdo, but founding father Charlie (Charles) Martel, an eighth-century Frankish warrior 'king' who defeated an Arab army at the Battle of Tours in 732 CE.
2. TF1, 'Vie politique', 11 September 2016, http://www.tf1.fr/tf1/vie-politique/videos/vie-politique-11-septembre-2016.html (last accessed 18 July 2017).
3. See Caroline Monnot and Abel Mestre, *Le Système Le Pen. Enquête sur les réseaux du Front national*, Paris: Denoël, 2011, p. 38.
4. See Marine Le Pen, *À contre flots*, Paris: Jacques Grancher, 2006, Chapter 1.
5. See Claude Askolovitch, 'Dynastie. Jean-Marie Le Pen et ses filles, une tragédie familiale', *Vanity Fair France*, 7 December 2015.
6. Le Pen, *À contre flots*, p. 89.
7. Ibid., p. 40.
8. Ibid., p. 45.

9. See Monnot and Mestre, *Le Système Le Pen*, p. 41.
10. See Patrice Machuret, *Dans la peau de Marine Le Pen*, Paris: Seuil, 2012, p. 185.
11. Laureline Dupont, 'Paul-Marie Coûteaux prof particulier de Marine Le Pen', *Le Point*, 20 February 2015.
12. Interview with the author.
13. Ibid.
14. Interview with the author.
15. Interview with the author.
16. See Patrice Machuret, *Dans la peau de Marine Le Pen*. Her acceptance speech as leader of the FN, delivered in Tours in January 2011, appeared to have undergone several rewritings: a first version by her brother-in-law Philippe Olivier, the addition of references to left-wing giant Jean Jaurès by Louis Aliot, a veneration of the State from Florian Philippot...

1. THE FOUR PILLARS OF THE FAR RIGHT

1. The FN took part in this far-right carnival from 1979 to 1988, after which the party began to organize its own separate celebration on 1 May.
2. Interview with the author.
3. Interview with the author.
4. The term '*image conductrice*' (driving image) originated with the Swiss academic Armin Mohler.
5. Immanuel Kant, *Toward Perpetual Peace and Other Writings on Politics, Peace, and History*, New Haven CT: Yale University Press, p. 82.
6. Carl Schmitt, *Land and Sea*, Berlin: Plutarch Press, 1997.
7. Ibid.
8. In his *Manifesto of Futurism* (1909), Filippo Tommaso

Marinetti (1876–1944) celebrated 'the aggressive movement', 'the slap' and 'the punch'. This vindication of violence in poetry, outside far-right circles, is also to be found among the French Surrealists or in the work of Vladimir Mayakovsky.

9. René Guénon (1886–1951), an Orientalist and esotericist who moved to Egypt in 1930, fought against modernity in the name of rites, symbols and initiations, notably in *La Crise du monde moderne* (*Crisis of the Modern World*, 1927).
10. See, for example, *Imperialismo pagano* (*Heathen Imperialism*) by the Italian philosopher Julius Evola (1898–1974).
11. A forgery produced in Paris in 1901 by an agent of the Okhrana, the Tsarist secret police, who plagiarized Maurice Joly's *Dialogue aux enfers entre Machiavel et Montesquieu* (*Dialogue in Hell Between Machiavelli and Montesquieu*), a satirical pamphlet describing a fictitious plan by Napoleon III to conquer the world.

2. DADDY'S FN

1. I lost my strength and my life,
   My friends and my joy;
   I lost till the pride
   That made my genius believable.
   When I knew Truth,
   I thought she was a friend;
   When I understood and felt her,
   I was already disgusted by her.
2. 'To be and to last' or 'To be and to hold out.'
3. In accordance with the ruling of the Nanterre High Court

on 17 November 2016, Jean-Marie Le Pen was excluded from membership of the FN, but remained honorary president of the party he founded.

3. THE HUMAN FACE OF NATIONALISM

1. *Rivarol*, 9 April 2015.
2. Interview with the author.
3. See Sylvain Crépon, Alexandre Dézé and Nonna Mayer (eds), *Les Faux-Semblants du Front national. Sociologie d'un parti politique*, Paris: Presses de Sciences Po, 2015, p. 28: 'It was out of another neologism—*diabolisation* [demonization]—that the term was coined at the end of the 1980s by the leadership of the Front National.'
4. See Dominique Albertini and David Doucet, *Histoire du Front national*, Paris: Tallandier, 2013, p. 32. Ordre nouveau replaced Occident, a far-right movement involved in violent street clashes with the far left in May 1968. It was banned and dissolved in October that year.
5. Interview with the author. The Organisation armée secrète (Secret Army Organisation) was a short-lived right-wing dissident paramilitary organization that carried out anti-independence terror attacks during the Algerian War (1954–62).
6. Le Pen referred to Michel Durafour as 'Mr Durafour-crématoire', a play on words as *four* is oven in French, and 'oven crematorium' is an allusion to the Nazi death camps of the Second World War.
7. A pro-Pétain song popular during the Vichy period of 1940–4.
8. Marine Le Pen, *À contre flots*, Paris: Jacques Grancher, 2006, p. 258.

9. Interview with the author.
10. *Le Point*, 3 February 2011.
11. *Le Figaro*, 8 June 2014.
12. Interview with the author.
13. *Libération*, 10 September 1996.
14. Speech, Paris, 10 December 2015.
15. *Le Point*, 9 September 2011.
16. Speech, Nantes, 25 March 2012.
17. *La Vie*, 16 June 2011. See also Le Pen, *À contre flots*, Chapter 4, where she is highly critical of the Catholic clergy: 'I would have sometimes liked to have found a little more neutrality, if not just restraint, among Church people', since 'many of them barred us from salvation on the grounds that you can't be a Catholic and a member of the Front National.'
18. Le Pen, *À contre flots*, Chapter 4.
19. Interview with the author.
20. May 1968 marked a highly significant period of civil unrest, involving massive general strikes, occupation of factories and universities and, ultimately, a political crisis at the very top of the Republic. 'May '68' is still a key social, political and cultural reference point, considered by many to be a revolutionary moment. It called into question both traditional political and social institutions and the values of consumerism, capitalism and 'Americanization' that emerged during the 'Trente Glorieuses' (three 'glorious' decades of rapid post-war growth that hugely boosted purchasing power and social mobility). François Mitterrand was the Socialist French president from 1981 to 1995.

21. See Albertini and Doucet, *Histoire du Front national*, p. 16.
22. As in the case, for instance, of Roger Holeindre, born in 1929, a former army volunteer in Indochina and Algeria and a member of the OAS, who left the FN after Marine Le Pen became party president. See Caroline Monnot and Abel Mestre, *Le Système Le Pen. Enquête sur les réseaux du Front national*, Paris: Denoël, 2011, p. 26.
23. Jean-Marie Le Pen, 'Le discours de La Trinité: démarxiser la France', *Présent*, 30 August 1991, cited in Maryse Souchard, Stéphane Wahnich, Isabelle Cuminal and Virginie Wathier, *Le Pen, les mots. Analyse d'un discours d'extrême droite*, Paris: La Découverte, 1997, p. 60.
24. Marine Le Pen, *Pour que vive la France*, Paris: Jacques Grancher, 2012, p. 106: 'I could, moreover, annoy him [political historian Pierre Rosanvallon] by arguing that Marx's internationalism does not consist of a hatred of nation states, but in reality of an international coordination of struggles led by the working classes in their national contexts.'
25. *Le Figaro*, 28 July 2016.
26. Speech, Paris, 1 May 2013.
27. Le Pen, *À contre flots*, p. 187.
28. Speech, Paris, 1 May 2016.
29. Ibid.
30. Speech, Paris, 1 May 2015. 'No need for a grotesque gender theory when you cut your hair and wear men's clothing.'
31. Ibid.
32. Speech, Châteauroux, 26 February 2012.
33. Collectif Racine, 'Appel pour le redressement de l'École',

2 May 2013, http://www.collectifracine.fr/blog/2013/05/02/appel-pour-le-redressement-de-lecole (last accessed 22 August 2017).

34. Audace, 'Notre charte', http://jeunesactifs-patriotes.fr/le-collectif/ (last accessed 22 August 2017).
35. Marine 2017, 'Reportage: Convention thématique sur la protection animale (11/10/16)', video report, 13 October 2016, https://www.youtube.com/watch?v=PzAwVEZf55M (last accessed 22 August 2017).
36. See Cécile Alduy and Stéphane Wahnich, *Marine Le Pen prise aux mots. Décryptage du nouveau discours frontiste*, Paris: Seuil, 2015, p. 34.
37. Interviews with the author.
38. Speech, Saint-Laurent-du-Var, 7 September 2010. Gaxotte (1895–1982) was secretary to Charles Maurras, founder of Action française.
39. Speech, Saint-Denis, 9 January 2012.
40. Speech, Metz, 12 December 2011.
41. The generic term for Muslim Algerians who served as auxiliaries in the French Army during the Algerian War.
42. Interview with the author. For 1968 and Mitterrand, see Chapter 3 note 20.
43. Speech, Metz, 12 December 2011.
44. Speech, Paris, 19 November 2011. 'Clemenceau said: "One must first know what one wants, have the courage to say so, and then have the energy to do it."'
45. Closing speech, Front National summer university, Marseille, 6 September 2015. 'Jules Ferry used to say: "School must be a sanctuary removed from the noise of society."'

46. Speech, Tours, 16 January 2011. '"The fatherland is all that is left to he who has nothing," said Jaurès.'
47. Speech, Saint-Denis, 9 January 2012. 'Let us cry out with Émile Zola that "the truth is on the march and nothing will stop it!"'
48. Speech, Paris, 19 November 2011. 'Albert Einstein had the right answer when he said that "we cannot solve our problems with the same thinking that created them."'
49. Speech, Oxford, 5 February 2015.
50. Ibid. 'I still recall these verses by Paul Éluard which illustrate the elusive notion marvellously: "And by the power of a word, I start my life again. I was born to know you, to name you. Freedom."'
51. Speech, Paris, 1 May 2016. 'I devote myself to what is essential. Thus "the essential is constantly threatened by the insignificant," as René Char said.'
52. Speech, Paris, 19 November 2011, presenting her presidential campaign. 'Those in power have made this Cocteau quote their own: "Those things are beyond us; let us pretend to have organized them."'
53. Speech, Oxford, 5 February 2015. 'Albert Camus said: "To misname things is to add to the world's woes."'
54. Speech, Nantes, 25 March 2012. 'All the children of France should be thrilled, like Marc Bloch, by the story of the coronations at Reims and the story of Valmy.' French kings were crowned in the cathedral at Reims; the Battle of Valmy against Prussia in 1792 was the first major victory by the French Army during the Revolutionary Wars that followed the French Revolution of 1789.
55. Speech, Marseille, 4 March 2012. 'As Hannah Arendt said

in a phrase that offers much food for thought: "Tradition alone makes authority."'

56. See Le Pen, *Pour que vive la France*, p. 112.
57. Speech, Fréjus, 17 September 2016.
58. Presidential rally, Bordeaux, 22 January 2012. '"If we want things to stay as they are, things will have to change." This famous retort from Visconti's *The Leopard* sums up in a few words French political life since 1970.'
59. Speech, Paris, 1 May 2011.
60. For instance, at her appearance at the Front National's summer university at La Baule, 26 September 2012: 'Let us begin, dear friends, with these admirable words from Michelet: "Frenchmen of all sorts, of all classes, of all parties, remember one thing, on this earth you have only one true friend, and that is France!"'
61. Interview with the author.
62. Speech, Nantes, 25 March 2012. Her position recalls that of the nationalist writer Maurice Barrès, who wrote in *La Terre et les morts* (Paris: L'Herne, 2016, p. 20). 'Do you not find it slightly puerile to head off, even along with eminent philosophers, into the hypothetical paths along which France should have passed? You will find greater reward in following the road that she really took.'
63. Speech, Paris, 19 November 2011.
64. Speech, Metz, 12 December 2011.
65. Speech, Paris, 1 May 2013. A reference to the first-century BC Gallic Wars, and to the French referendum which rejected a treaty establishing a Constitution of the European Union.
66. Speech, Marseille, 15 September 2013. 'This is why I will place the teaching of French history at the centre of syl-

labuses. Nicolas Sarkozy had got rid of Charles Martel, Henri IV, Louis XIV and Napoleon, and now François Hollande is removing General de Gaulle.'

67. Speech, Paris, 1 May 2011. Free France was the name of de Gaulle's London-based government-in-exile during the Vichy years (1940–4).
68. Speech, 'Seminar on Defence', 3 December 2011.
69. Ibid.
70. Interview with the author.
71. Interview with the author.
72. Interview with the author.
73. The Russian president intervened—unprecedentedly—in the right's primaries for the 2017 presidential election, to support François Fillon. Between this and the FN, he had two irons in the fire for 2017, while on 2 December 2016 *Le Monde* ran the headline 'European elections and cyberwarfare: German and French governments concerned over destabilization of 2017 polling by Russia.'

4. A TOTALITARIAN UNIVERSE

1. Speech, Paris, 1 May 2013. 'We are at war with all the totalitarianisms of the twenty-first century—above all, globalism and fundamentalist Islamism!'
2. Louis Aliot, interview with the author.
3. See, for example, Cédric Lagandré, *La Société intégrale*, Paris: Climats, 2009, or Dany-Robert Dufour, *L'Individu qui vient... après le libéralisme*, Paris: Denoël, 2011. It should be made clear that these authors have nothing to do with the FN.
4. Speech, Paris, 1 May 2011.
5. Ibid.

6. Speech, Tours, 16 January 2011.
7. Speech, Paris, 19 November 2011. 'Democracy in France expresses itself at the national level, not through supranational authorities that have nothing democratic about them.'
8. Ibid.
9. Claude Lefort, 'La logique totalitaire' (1980), in Enzo Traverso (ed.), *Le Totalitarisme. Le XXe siècle en débat*, Paris: Seuil, 2001, p. 719: 'Only the state appears to all and represents itself as the founding principle, as the great actor which holds the means of social transformation and of knowledge of all things. It is the advent of "the state's perspective" ... that makes possible *the formidable expansion of bureaucracies, whose members can cultivate their own interests and each extract the maximum possible power and advantages, while using as a pretext their sovereign distance in respect of the electorate*.' Emphasis added.
10. Speech, Tours, 16 January 2011.
11. Speech, Paris, 19 November 2011.
12. Ibid.
13. Ibid. This argument was reinforced by the announcement in September 2016 of investment bank Goldman Sachs' appointment of the former president of the European Commission, José Manuel Barroso (2004–14).
14. Marine Le Pen, *Pour que vive la France*, Paris: Jacques Grancher, 2012, p. 98. 'International forums like the Mont Pelerin Society, the Bilderberg Group or the Davos forum are not places where dark plots are hatched. They are simply melting pots of politicians and bankers from the right and left, which allow the winners within the system to exchange ideas and information. Simply because

they connive as a group, they cultivate the same ideology for the future, that of allegedly free competition in a free market and that of global governance.'

15. Speech, Paris, 19 November 2011.
16. Ibid.
17. Ibid.
18. Ibid. Marine Le Pen's anti-Semitic audience will find some familiar motifs here. Submission to the idol of money, in contrast with the true Christian faith, is one of the obligatory themes of religious anti-Judaism and social anti-Semitism. See, for example, Édouard Drumont, *La France juive*, Paris: C. Marpon and E. Flammarion, 1886, pp. 3–4: '"The Jew follows the cult of money." This statement of an obvious fact still sounds overinflated in the mouths of most who make it. And yet look at those great lords, those pious ladies, those regulars at Sainte-Clotilde and Saint-Thomas-d'Aquin who go after church to bow and scrape before a Rothschild who regards their adored Christ as the vilest of imposters. What brings these representatives of the nobility under his roof? Reverence for money. What are they going there to do? Kneel before the golden calf.'
19. Speech, Metz, 12 December 2011.
20. Ibid.
21. Ibid.
22. See Cécile Alduy and Stéphane Wahnich, *Marine Le Pen prise aux mots. Décryptage du nouveau discours frontiste*, Paris: Seuil, 2015, p. 152.
23. Nicolas Lebourg, *Le Monde vu de la plus extrême droite. Du fascisme au nationalisme révolutionnaire*, Perpignan: Presses universitaires de Perpignan, 2010, p. 172.

24. Speech, Paris, 19 November 2011.
25. Speech, Bompas, 11 March 2012.
26. Speech, Rouen, 15 January 2012.
27. Le Pen, *Pour que vive la France*, p. 27. See Gilles Lipovetsky, *L'Ère du vide*, Paris: Gallimard, 1983.
28. Speech, Bordeaux, 22 January 2012. The CAC 40 is a benchmark French stock market index, the equivalent of the UK's FTSE 100 or the Dow Jones.
29. Speech, Paris, 1 May 2011.
30. Speech, Marseille, 6 September 2015.
31. George Orwell, *1984*, quoted in Le Pen, *Pour que vive la France*, p. 109.
32. Speech, Tours, 16 January 2011.
33. An economic and social theorist, writer, political adviser and senior civil servant, who served as a counsellor to President Mitterrand from 1981 to 1991 and was the first head of the European Bank for Reconstruction and Development in 1991–3.
34. Speech, Paris, 19 November 2011. See Jacques Attali, *Demain, qui gouvernera le monde?*, Paris: Fayard, 2011. See also Daniele Archibugi, *La Démocratie cosmopolitique. Sur la voie d'une démocratie mondiale*, Paris: Éditions du Cerf, 2009.
35. Speech, Marseille, 6 September 2015.
36. Le Pen, *Pour que vive la France*, p. 77.
37. Speech, Paris, 19 November 2011.
38. Hannah Arendt, *Totalitarianism, Part Three of The Origins of Totalitarianism*, New York: Houghton Mifflin Harcourt, 1968, p. 172.
39. Ibid., p. 173.
40. Ibid.

41. Speech, Paris, 19 November 2011.
42. Ibid.
43. See, for example, Speech, Bordeaux, 22 January 2012. 'The forgotten for whom I fight are the working poor, shopkeepers, artisans, office workers, manual workers, the middle classes, those left behind in the countryside, the retired, the unemployed young or old; the France that has disdainfully been called "lesser France", sometimes "stale France".'
44. Alain Finkielkraut, *L'Identité malheureuse*, Paris: Gallimard, 2013.
45. See Charles Péguy, *Notes conjointes sur M. Descartes et la philosophie cartésienne*, in *OEuvres en prose complètes*, Paris: Gallimard, 'Bibliothèque de la Pléiade', vol. 3, p. 1431: 'It is from there that this immense prostitution of the modern world came. It did not originate in lust. It is not even worthy of that. It comes from money. It comes from this universal interchangeability.'
46. Speech, Paris, 1 May 2013.
47. Interview with the far-right publication *Réfléchir et agir*, winter 2014, p. 32.
48. Speech, Paris, 19 November 2011.
49. Ibid.
50. One chapter in *Pour que vive la France* is entitled 'Ultraliberal Metaphysics'. It starts with an epigraph by Dany-Robert Dufour: 'Perhaps it is time we noticed that capitalism is based on ... a metaphysics whose power no longer needs to be proven, as it has succeeded in taking over the world.' (Dany-Robert Dufour, *Le Divin Marché*, Paris: Denoël, 2007).
51. Speech, Tours, 16 January 2011.

52. Speech, Pontoise, 30 November 2011. Le Pen was addressing that year's fairground trade fair.
53. Speech, Marseille, 6 September 2015.
54. Speech, Châteauroux, 26 February 2012.
55. See Renaud Camus, *La Grande Déculturation*, Paris: Fayard, 2008.
56. Speech, Metz, 12 December 2011.
57. In Le Pen, *Pour que vive la France*, p. 134.
58. See Jean Baudrillard, *Simulacres et simulation*, Paris: Galilée, 1981. See, for example, his analysis of Disneyland, 'presented as imaginary in order to make us believe that the rest is real', 'a deterrence machine set up as an opposition in order to rejuvenate the fiction of the real', when in reality it is the world that is fake.
59. Aleksandr Dugin, *The Fourth Political Theory*, London: Arktos Media, 2012.
60. Ibid.
61. Ibid.
62. Speech, Châteauroux, 26 February 2012.
63. Alain de Benoist's GRECE, hostile to political and economic liberalism, stood in opposition to the Club de l'horloge, conservative but liberal. See Jean-Yves Camus, 'Le Front national et la Nouvelle Droite', in Sylvain Crépon, Alexandre Dézé and Nonna Mayer (eds), *Les Faux-Semblants du Front national. Sociologie d'un parti politique*, Paris: Presses de Sciences Po, 2015, p. 97.
64. The term is Alain de Benoist's, leading light of GRECE and its journals (*Éléments*, *Krisis*, *Nouvelle École*).
65. This idea of protecting difference was advanced by the anthropologist Claude Lévi-Strauss in his 1971 *Race et Culture*. In this polemical text Lévi-Strauss laments that

'the upheavals unleashed by an expanding industrial civilization, the increasing speed of modes of transport and communication' are leading 'humanity towards a global civilization, destructive of the old particularisms honoured for having created the spiritual and aesthetic values that give life its meaning, and which we preciously collect in libraries and museums.' Thus, 'all true creation implies a certain deafness to the appeal of other values' and 'one cannot immerse oneself in the pleasure of the other' if one wishes to remain dynamic. Those who support differentialism often refer to this text, and Marine Le Pen quoted Lévi-Strauss in her speech at Fréjus, 17 September 2016.

66. Speech, Fréjus, 17 September 2016.
67. Caroline Monnot and Abel Mestre, *Le Système Le Pen. Enquête sur les réseaux du Front national*, Paris: Denoël, 2011, p. 48.
68. Ibid., p. 48.
69. Dugin, *The Fourth Political Theory*.
70. Speech, Valdai Discussion Club, 27 October 2016, available in the original Russian at Kremlin.ru/events/president/news/53151 (last accessed 24 August 2017): 'People don't vote at all how they were advised to by the official and respectable media and by the parties of the system. As for social movements, until recently considered "too far to the left" or "too far to the right", they took centre stage.'
71. Speech, Brachay, 3 September 2016. 'Our project turns its back on the ephemeral, the superficial, the outwardly visible, in favour of what is durable and sincere.'
72. Speech, Paris, 1 May 2013.

73. From 2007 to 2012, the symbol of this elitist impropriety was, in her eyes, Nicolas Sarkozy: 'A pleasure-seeking president, an unfettered president, Nicolas Sarkozy very quickly degraded his office and demonstrated to an astounded French people the daily indecency of his behaviour. Disrespectful of republican norms, disrespectful towards institutions and, more seriously, towards the French themselves, from the beginning of his term he gave the impression of a president unfit for office.' Speech, Toulouse, 5 February 2012.
74. See Bruce Bégout, *De la décence ordinaire. Court essai sur une idée fondamentale de la pensée politique de George Orwell*, Paris: Allia, 2008, and Jean-Claude Michéa, *Orwell, anarchiste Tory*, Paris: Climats, 2008.
75. Speech, Brachay, 3 September 2016.
76. Interview with the author.

5. THE REPUBLICAN TURN

1. Literally, 'let the whore die', a traditional royalist insult directed at the Republic.
2. Manuel Valls was François Hollande's prime minister from 2014 to 2016.
3. TNS Sofres, 'Baromètre d'image du Front national 2016' (poll on the FN's image for *Le Monde*, France Info and Canal Plus),. http://www.tns-sofres. com/sites/default/files/2016.02.05-baro-fn.pdf (last accessed 24 August 2017).
4. In the regional elections of 2015, the FN received 27.7 per cent of votes in the first round. The percentage decreased in the second round (27.4 per cent) but only because of greater turnout. In terms of number of votes,

the party progressed and received, according to FN specialist Alexandre Dézé, 'more votes than the party [had] ever polled at the end of an election: 6.8 million.' Yet despite this progression, it has been unable to obtain a single regional president. See Alexandre Dézé, *Comprendre le Front national*, Paris: Bréal, 2016, p. 25.

5. Speech, Paris, 19 November 2011.
6. Speech, Merdrignac, Brittany, 20 April 2012. 'On 2 March, on the occasion of the Agricultural Show, I opened up and read the grievance lists of the rural world, of agriculture and of fishing. I have not stopped collecting and noting these grievances throughout the campaign. Today I want to be the voice of those whom our elites refuse to listen to.' The *cahiers de doléances* were the lists of grievances drawn up by each of the three Estates in France, between March and April 1789, the year in which revolution began.
7. Cécile Alduy and Stéphane Wahnich, *Marine Le Pen prise aux mots. Décryptage du nouveau discours frontiste*, Paris: Seuil, 2015, p. 48.
8. Speech, Paris, 19 November 2011. 'In 2005, we expressed our thirst for democracy, for freedom, for France. It was the referendum on the European constitution and the glorious French "no", I'm sure you remember: that "no", filled with hope, that "no" that shook the political, economic and media caste, and which struck horror into the trading rooms.'
9. Speech, Paris, 16 January 2011. 'As in the most critical moments in her history, France is facing the threat of falling apart.'

10. Speech, Joan of Arc Day, Paris, 1 May 2013. Emphasis added.
11. See Dézé, *Comprendre le Front national*, p. 70.
12. Presidential investiture speech, FN Congress, Tours 16 January 2011.
13. Marine Le Pen, *Pour que vive la France*, Paris: Jacques Grancher, 2012, p. 32. She even claims that the financial powers 'have de facto re-established the debt bondage that was abolished by King Solomon in 500 BC'. (Speech, Paris, 19 November 2011).
14. Speech, Tours, 16 January 2011.
15. Speech, Paris, 19 November 2011.
16. Ibid. 'From the very start of my five-year term in office, I will invite the French people to speak out on important reforms to the Constitution. Among the democratic advances that I will ask the French to ratify are a move to a non-renewable seven-year presidential term, a ban on revising the Constitution other than by consultation with the people as a whole and the adoption of referendums through popular initiative.'
17. Speech, Tours, 16 January 2011. 'The nation state must again impose itself, by sorting out its objectives and methods. This national choice that I will make with you demands from us a great reordering of the nation state. In a country where the nation has been built through the will of the state, the one does not work without the other.'
18. A term applied to supporters of the right-wing populist Pierre Poujade (1920–2003), whose Defence Union of Shopkeepers and Craftsmen won fifty-two seats in parliament in 1956, including that of Jean-Marie Le Pen.
19. Alduy and Wahnich, *Marine Le Pen prise aux mots*, p. 42.

20. The doctrine of a sovereigntist, non-federal French state outside the EU, espoused by Jean-Pierre Chevènement, a former Socialist minister who contested the 2002 presidential election.
21. Speech, Paris, 19 November 2011.
22. Speech, Marseille, 4 March 2012.
23. Speech, Tours, 16 January 2011.
24. See Caroline Monnot and Abel Mestre, *Le Système Le Pen. Enquête sur les réseaux du Front national*, Paris: Denoël, 2011, p. 167.
25. Speech, Paris, 19 November 2011.
26. Ibid.
27. Interview with the author.
28. A fictional travel book by Augustine Fouillée, published in 1877 and widely used in the schools of the Third Republic, where it was influential for generations of children in creating a sense of a unified French nation.
29. Speech, Paris, 1 May 2011. 'The restoration of education will take place through a rise in standards, in teacher training but also in the classroom: rising standards in attainment, rising standards in discipline, rising standards in the transmission of values. ... An appreciation of effort, of republican virtue, of hard work will be rewarded.'
30. Speech, Marseille, 4 March 2012.
31. Speech, Nantes, 25 March 2012.
32. Quoted in Le Pen, *Pour que vive la France*, p. 158. See also her homage in the special edition of *Le Monde* dedicated to Victor Hugo, February 2012, pp. 81–2.
33. Quoted notably in Le Pen, *Pour que vive la France*, pp. 7, 124.
34. Pierre Rosanvallon, *Le Peuple introuvable. Histoire de la*

représentation démocratique en France, Paris: Gallimard, 2002, p. 137.

35. Notably in Gustave Le Bon's *Psychologie des foules*, 1895. An English translation, *The Crowd*, appeared in 1896 (London: Macmillan).
36. Zeev Sternhell, *Ni droite ni gauche. L'idéologie fasciste en France*, Paris: Gallimard, 2012, p. 230.
37. Michel Winock, *Nationalisme, antisémitisme et fascisme en France*, Paris: Seuil, 2014, p. 193.
38. Interview with the author.

6. NEITHER RIGHT NOR LEFT

1. Alain, *Propos*, December 1930.
2. Speech, Reims, 17 February 2014.
3. 'I belong to the right, and I am not going to change now. In the 1960s, nobody wanted to admit to being right-wing. Jean Lecanuet defined his party, the UDF, as 'centre-left', and Jacques Chirac, when he founded the RPR, presented it as 'a French version of Labourism', even though Labourism is the socialism of Anglo-Saxon countries. We picked the epithet of the right out of the gutter. That was the cause of our demonization. We alone, indeed, dared to challenge the moral authority that the left had conferred on itself and before which everyone bowed down.' Interview with the author.
4. See Institut national de l'audiovisuel (INA) archives, 3 November 1972. He repudiated the designation of the party as far-right, even while admitting that the far right was one of the FN's component parts. He preferred it to be labelled as 'right or national opposition'.

5. Cited in Dominique Albertini and David Doucet, *Histoire du Front national*, Paris: Tallandier, 2013, p. 51.
6. Ibid.
7. Interview with the author.
8. An industrial suburb of Dunkerque, scene of a devastating fire in a migrant camp in April 2017.
9. See Renaud Dély, 'Au FN, le slogan "ni droite ni gauche" entretient les querelles', *Libération*, 19 February 1996, and Vincent Riou, 'Maréchal, te revoilà!', *Society*, no. 6, May 2015.
10. Speech, Metz, 12 December 2011.
11. Marine Le Pen, *Pour que vive la France*, Paris: Jacques Grancher, 2012, p. 147. On May 1968, see Chapter 3 note 20.
12. Ibid., p. 149.
13. See Sylvain Crépon, Alexandre Dézé and Nonna Mayer (eds), *Les Faux-Semblants du Front national. Sociologie d'un parti politique*, Paris: Presses de Sciences Po, 2015, p. 36.
14. See Cécile Alduy and Stéphane Wahnich, *Marine Le Pen prise aux mots*, Paris: Seuil, 2015, p. 40.
15. Speech, Paris, 1 May 2011.
16. Speech, Rouen, 15 January 2012: 'I only want to talk about the France of the forgotten.'
17. Speech, Saint-Denis, 9 January 2012.
18. Interview with the author.
19. Speech, Paris, 19 November 2011.
20. Ibid.
21. Presidential meeting, Bordeaux, 22 January 2012.
22. Speech, Paris, 19 November 2011.
23. Le Pen, *Pour que vive la France*, p. 113.

24. Ibid., p. 112.
25. Ibid.
26. Jean-Michel Michéa, *Les Mystéres de la gauche. De l'idéal des Lumières au triomphe du capitalisme absolu*, Paris: Flammarion, 'Champs Essais', 2013.
27. Ibid., 2014 edition, pp. 15–16.
28. Ibid., p. 46.
29. Ibid., pp. 50–51. Emphasis in original.
30. The *bête immonde*, a phrase normally ascribed to Bertolt Brecht, but in fact coined as 'vile beast' by Hoffman Reynold Hays, American translator of *The Resistible Rise of Arturo Ui*, as a metaphor for fascism or Nazism. The phrase was subsequently used in the French translation of the play.
31. Michéa, *Les Mystères de la gauche* (2014), p. 51.
32. Zeev Sternhell, *Ni droite ni gauche. L'idéologie fasciste en France*, Paris: Gallimard, 'Folio histoire', 4th ed., 2012.
33. Ibid., p. 230.
34. Maurice Barrès, 'The Cult of the Self', not available in English translation.
35. Maurice Barrès, 'Le flot qui monte', *Le Courrier de l'Est*, 26 May 1889, quoted in Zeev Sternhell, *Maurice Barrès et le nationalisme français*, Paris: Fayard, 2016, p. 186, note 1.
36. Sternhell, *Maurice Barrès et le nationalisme français*, p. 187.
37. Georges Sorel, *Réflexions sur la violence*, Chapter 1, I, Paris: Marcel Rivière et Cie, 1972, available at http://dx.doi.org/doi:10.1522/cla.sog.ref.
38. Ibid., Chapter 2, II.
39. Ibid., Chapter 1, II.

40. The Confédération générale du travail (General Confederation of Labour), France's second largest trade union, was founded in 1895 and, at the time of Sorel's book, anarcho-syndicalist in outlook.
41. Sorel, *Réflexions sur la violence*, Chapter 1, II.
42. Ibid., Chapter 2, II.
43. Ibid., Chapter 2, II.
44. He notably refers to 'the fat Jewish bankers' who know how to 'dazzle' 'Jaurès and his friends' (ibid., Chapter 1, I).
45. Sorel, *Réflexions sur la violence*, Chapter 4, I.
46. Ibid.
47. Pierre-Joseph Proudhon (1809–65), a leading figure in French socialism and a rival of Marx, supported a national and federalist socialism. He was the author of notebooks dotted with anti-Semitic remarks. Even today, he is commemorated in Alain de Benoist's journal *Éléments* and on the anti-Semitic website 'Égalité et Réconciliation' run by Alain Soral—whose pseudonym is reminiscent of a certain Sorel.
48. Georges Navet, 'Le Cercle Proudhon (1911–1914). Entre le syndicalisme révolutionnaire et l'Action française, *Mil neuf cent*, vol. 10, no. 1, 1992, p. 53.
49. Quoted in Michel Winock, *Nationalisme, antisémitisme et fascism en France*, Paris: Seuil, 2014, p. 243.
50. See Zeev Sternhell, Mario Sznajder and Maia Ashéri, *Naissance de l'idéologie fasciste*, Paris: Gallimard, 'Folio histoire', 2010.
51. An alliance of left-wing parties, including the French Communist Party and socialists, which formed a government from 1936 to 1938.

52. Section Française de l'Internationale Ouvrière (French Section of the Workers' International (SFIO), founded in 1905 and precursor of the French Communist Party and Socialist Party.
53. One of the principal collaborationist parties under the Vichy regime.
54. Groupe union défense, a far-right student organization; see Introduction.
55. See Serge Ayoub, *Doctrine du solidarisme*, Saint-Denis: Éditions du Pont d'Arcole, 2012.
56. See Caroline Monnot and Abel Mestre, *Le Système Le Pen. Enquête sur les réseaux du Front national*, Paris: Denoël, 2011, p. 29.

7. THE ENEMY WITHIN

1. Interview with the author.
2. 'The Daughter as De-demonizer', *Haaretz*, 7 January 2011.
3. *Le Figaro*, 8 June 2014.
4. '"Détail de l'histoire": Marine Le Pen en "désaccord profond" avec son père', *Le Monde*, 3 April 2015.
5. TF1, 9 April 2015, interview with Gilles Bouleau.
6. See Marine Le Pen, *À contre flots*, Paris: Jacques Grancher, 2006, p. 91.
7. Speech, Paris, 19 November 2011.
8. Édouard Drumont, *La France juive*, Paris: C. Marpon and E. Flammarion, 1886, p. 7.
9. Ibid., pp. 8–9.
10. Speech, Paris, 19 November 2011.
11. Ibid.
12. Drumont, *La France juive*, Introduction, p. vi.

13. A high-profile philosopher and media personality of Algerian Jewish origin.
14. A traditional French dance similar to a gavotte.
15. Speech, Metz, 12 December 2011.
16. Speech, Toulouse, 5 February 2012.
17. Ibid.
18. Alain Soral, *Comprendre l'empire. Demain la gouvernance globale ou la révolte des nations?*, Paris: Éditions Blanche, 2011, p. 38. Here, the author takes up many obligatory themes of the far-right anti-Semitic tradition: 'money's seizure of power' with the advent of the 'Judeo-Protestant' 'bourgeois mentality' after the revolution of 1789; the growing influence of freemasonry (whose symbol is not 'the Pantheon of the Greeks' but 'the temple of Solomon'); a fascination with 'the occultism and co-optation through initiation' of 'networks, lobbies, pressure groups'. The book abounds with Judeophobic attacks—'the contemptuous inegalitarianism of the Old Testament'; 'Jewish elites ... often driven by a vengeful messianism' (p. 69); 'a pluri-millennial faith founded on the clearly established project of domination'—and anti-Semitic circumlocutions: 'Two banking principles co-exist in the West, one Protestant and somewhat ascetic and entrepreneurial in form, the other more difficult to define and speculative' (p. 45). After pillorying the Crif (the Conseil représentatif des institutions juives de France, an umbrella of French Jewish organizations), 'where the entire French government, led by the president of the Republic, goes to receive its orders at an annual dinner from a community representing less than 1 per cent of the French population', Soral even condemns 'an oligarchy of scarcely

1 per cent of the population that has always commanded the remaining 99 per cent; like a pack of wolves dominating a flock of sheep'.

19. Ibid., p. 47.
20. Speech, Toulouse, 5 February 2012.
21. Marine Le Pen, *Pour que vive la France*, Paris: Jacques Grancher, 2012, p. 119.
22. Speech, Toulouse, 5 February 2012. Emphasis added.
23. Interview with the author.
24. Maghrebian garment covering part of the face.
25. Ibid.
26. Ibid.
27. Ibid.
28. See Patrice Machuret, *Dans la peau de Marine Le Pen*, Paris: Seuil, 2012, pp. 124–5. 'He made clear his satisfaction at seeing his "family line" confirmed. Asked the following week about his daughter's choice of terminology, Le Pen was pleased with himself: "It's true, I must say I'm rather satisfied by it."'
29. Speech, La Baule, 26 September 2012.
30. Reuters France, 'Les musulmans doivent payer pour leurs mosques, dit Le Pen', 19 December 2010, http://fr.reuters.com/article/topNews/idFRPAE6BI0L720101219 (last accessed 25 August 2017).
31. 'Ce n'est pas l'islam qui pose problem, mais sa visibilité', *Zaman France*, available at http://www.gerard-brazon.com/article-marine-le-pen-video-ce-n-est-pas-l-islam-qui-pose-probleme-mais-sa-visibilite-116775312.html (last accessed 25 August 2017)
32. B.D. and AFP, 'Marine Le Pen: "Les anti-Semites sont dans les quartiers"', *20 Minutes*, 19 March 2014, http://

www.20minutes.fr/politique/1327690–20140319-marine-pen-antisemites-quartiers (last accessed 25 August 2017).

33. Interview with the author, *Philosophie Magazine*, no. 90, June 2015.
34. Speech, Rouen, 15 January 2012.
35. Ibid.
36. Speech, Tours, 16 January 2011.
37. Ibid.
38. Interview with the author.
39. Speech, Paris, 1 May 2015.
40. Speech, La Baule, 26 September 2012.
41. Speech, Nantes, 25 March 2012.
42. Speech, Reims, 17 February 2014.
43. Charles Maurras, *Comment je suis devenu royaliste*, n.d., available at http://maurras.net/textes/32.html (last accessed 25 August 2017).
44. Speech, Nantes, 25 March 2012. Mohamed Merah was responsible for the terrorist murders of seven people in Toulouse and Montauban in March 2012. He was killed by police in the same month.
45. Speech, Marseille, 6 September 2015.
46. Renaud Camus, *Abécédaire de l'innocence*, Neuilly-sur-Seine: Éditions David Reinharc, 2010.
47. Speech, Tours, 16 January 2011.
48. Press conference, Nanterre, 21 February 2011.
49. Speech, Six-Fours, 12 March 2011.
50. Speech, Fréjus, 17 September 2016.
51. Speech, Bordeaux, 22 January 2012.
52. Julien Dray, a Socialist politician and former leader of SOS Racisme.

53. Speech, Paris, 10 December 2015. The pun links the invented acronym ROM, short for Union of Globalist Organizations, with the French term for the Roma people (*les Roms*).

8. TILTING THE WORLD

1. This is the world envisaged by Immanuel Kant in his *Towards Perpetual Peace*.
2. Speech, Paris, 19 November 2011.
3. Dominique Albertini and David Doucet, *Histoire du Front national*, Paris: Tallandier, 2013, p. 118.
4. See Nicolas Lebourg, *Le Monde vu de la plus extrême droite. Du fascisme au nationalisme révolutionnaire*, Perpignan: Presses universitaires de Perpignan, 2010, pp. 47, 172.
5. Speech, Marseille, 15 September 2013.
6. Speech, Fréjus, 17 September 2016.
7. Speech, Marseille, 15 September 2013.
8. Speech, Paris, 19 November 2011.
9. Speech, Marseille, 15 September 2013.
10. Seminar on Defence, 3 December 2011.
11. Speech, Nantes, 25 March 2012.
12. Speech, Marseille, 4 March 2012.
13. Seminar on Defence, 3 December 2011.
14. See Albertini and Doucet, *Histoire du Front national*, p. 84: 'Stirbois, a partisan of French Algeria, was anti-Arab and pro-Israeli. Those emulating the Holocaust denier Duprat, meanwhile, admired the nationalist and authoritarian regimes in Egypt or Syria.' (François Duprat, a founding member of the Front National, was part of its

leadership until his still unexplained assassination in a car bomb attack in 1978.)

15. Sylvain Crépon, Alexandre Dézé and Nonna Mayer (eds), *Les Faux-Semblants du Front national. Sociologie d'un parti politique*, Paris: Presses de Sciences Po, 2015, pp. 65–7.
16. Ibid., p. 66.
17. Speech, Brachay, 3 September 2016.
18. Speech, Marseille, 15 September 2013.
19. Marine Turchi, 'Le travail d'influence des Émirats arabes unis auprès de Marine Le Pen', *Mediapart*, 21 October 2016.
20. *Le Point*, 13 October 2011.
21. Marine Turchi, 'Au Front national, le lobbying prorusse s'accélère', *Mediapart*, 18 December 2014: 'The Front National's Russophile line didn't start with Marine Le Pen. Her father already advocated a "Europe of nations from Brest to Vladivostok" and visited Russia as soon as "it was no longer communist". He formed solid friendships within nationalist circles and identified "common interests and enemies".'
22. See the Kremlin website, '70th session of the UN General Assembly', 28 September 2015, http://en.kremlin.ru/events/president/news/50385 (last accessed 31 August 2017).
23. Speech, Paris, 1 May 2016.
24. Turchi, 'Au Front national, le lobbying prorusse s'accélère'.
25. Ibid.: 'On 14 April, Marine Le Pen went back to Russia ... She insisted that "sanctions are counter-productive".'
26. Ibid.
27. Speech, Paris, 19 November 2011.

28. Ibid.
29. Interview with the author.
30. This politics of influence is now well documented in French. See Cécile Vaissié, *Les Réseaux du Kremlin en France*, Paris: Éditions Les Petits Matins, 2016, and Nicolas Hénin, *La France russe. Enquête sur les réseaux Poutine*, Paris: Fayard, 2016.
31. Éric Zemmour, *Le Suicide français*, Paris: Albin Michel, 2014.
32. Speech, Valdai Discussion Club, 19 September 2013. The Russian president clarified his thinking on the consequences of this apparent rejection: 'Policies are put into practice that put on the same level a family with several children and a same-sex partnership, or belief in God and belief in Satan. The excesses of political correctness are leading to a situation where serious consideration is given to allowing a political party whose aim is paedophile propaganda. People in many European countries are ashamed and scared of talking about their religious affiliation…'
33. Interview in the Austrian daily newspaper *Kurier*, '"Putin verteidigt Europas Zivilisation": Marine Le Pen will Frankenreich aus der EU führen und lobt Russlands Präsidenten.', 25 May 2014, https://kurier.at/politik/ausland/marine-le-pen-putin-verteidigt-die-werte-der-europaeischen-zivilisation/65.991.041 (last accessed 29 August 2017).
34. Putin, Boris Yeltsin's chosen successor, won two successive electoral mandates (200–4, 2004–8) before giving way to his protégé Dmitry Medvedev, for whom he served as prime minister while assuming the role of 'national leader' (2008–12). Returned to the presidency with a six-

year mandate (2012–18), he can also set his sights on a fourth mandate, up until 2024.

35. Speech, Saint-Laurent-du-Var, 7 September 2010.
36. Speech, La Baule, 26 September 2012.
37. Speech, Oxford, 5 February 2015.
38. G.W.F. Hegel, *Principes de la philosophie du droit* (*Elements of the Philosophy of Right*), 3, III § 324, Paris: Presses universitaires de France, 1988 (trans. Jean-François Kervégan'), p. 400.
39. See 'L'argent russe du Front national', *Mediapart*, 2 November 2015, https://www.mediapart.fr/journal/france/dossier/dossier-largent-russe-du-front-national (last accessed 29 August 2017).
40. The war between Assad and anti-regime rebels claimed more than 300,000 lives between its outbreak in 2011 and 13 September 2016, according to the Syrian Observatory for Human Rights.

9. HAS THE FN CHANGED?

1. See Alexandre Dézé, *Comprendre le Front national*, Paris: Bréal, 2016, p. 65.
2. Fyodor Dostoyevsky, *Notes from Underground*, Hastings: Delphi Classics, 2017 [original Russian 1864], Ch. 7.
3. Cécile Alduy and Stéphane Wahnich, *Marine Le Pen prise aux mots. Décryptage du nouveau discours frontiste*, Paris: Seuil, 2015, p. 41.
4. Maurice Barrès, *La Terre et les morts*, Paris: L'Herne, 2016, pp. 15–16.
5. Speech, Châteauroux, 26 February 2012.
6. Barrès, *La Terre et les morts*, p. 46.
7. Speech, Châteauroux, 26 February 2012.

8. Ibid.
9. Ibid.
10. Ibid. The adjective used by Lévy is *indécrottable*, implying both 'incorrigible' and, more literally, 'impossible to clean'.
11. Ibid.
12. Barrès, *La Terre et les morts*, p. 37.
13. Speech, Tours, 16 January 2011.
14. Speech, Saint-Laurent-du-Var, 7 September 2010.
15. Speech, Châteauroux, 26 February 2012.
16. It is worth noting that a German philosopher of the twentieth century also proposed an ontological theory of rootedness. Martin Heidegger, who was involved in Nazism, wrote an article in 1933 entitled 'Why Do We Stay in the Provinces?' extolling his 'age-old rootedness' in 'Swabian and Germanic' soil.
17. Maurice Barrès, *Les Déracinés*, Paris: Bartillat, 2010, p. 24.
18. Ibid., p. 24.
19. Ibid., p. 33.
20. Ibid., p. 34.
21. Barrès, *La Terre et les morts*, p. 42.
22. Speech, Châteauroux, 26 February 2012.
23. Speech, Marseille, 6 September 2015.
24. Ibid.
25. Ibid.
26. Ibid.
27. See, for example, Patrick Weil, *La France et ses étrangers. L'aventure d'une politique de l'immigration de 1938 à nos jours*, Paris: Gallimard, 'Folio histoire', 2005.
28. See 'Une frontière doit être ouverte ou fermée', *Philosophie Magazine*, no. 94, November 2015.

29. The polemicist Édouard Drumont is one of the precursors of an antipathy towards the open-minded, and hence (according to him) anti-popular, bourgeois: 'It was the bourgeois element ... that was primarily savage during the Commune, *the perverted and bohemian bourgeoisie from the Latin Quarter*; the people, in the midst of this dreadful crisis, remained *humane, that is to say French*.' Emphasis added. Cited in Georges Sorel, *Réflexions sur la violence*, Chapter 3, II. It seems, then, that the anti-Semitic Drumont was the ancestor of the ironic and pejorative concept of the 'bobo' (bohemian bourgeois).
30. Speech, Paris, 1 May 2015.
31. Barrès, *La Terre et les morts*, p. 33.
32. Speech, Paris, 1 May 2015.
33. Ibid.
34. Ibid.
35. François-René de Chateaubriand, 'De Buonaparte, des Bourbons et des Alliés' (1814), cited in Marine Le Pen's speech, Saint-Laurent-du-Var, 7 September 2010.
36. Speech, Paris, 19 November 2011.
37. Ibid.
38. Ibid.
39. Speech, Paris, 1 May 2011. Later that year, she declared: 'It is time for the spirit of France, from the Latin *spiritus*, the breath of France, to take new life' (speech, Paris, 19 November 2011).
40. Speech, Paris, 1 May 2013.
41. Speech, Paris, 1 May 2015.
42. Speech, Toulouse, 5 February 2012.
43. Speech, Paris, 1 May 2011.
44. Speech, Saint-Laurent-du-Var, 7 September 2010.

45. Ibid.
46. *Charnel*, otherwise translated as 'corporeal' or 'physical', but with a strong overtone of sensuality. See Robert Redeker, 'Reflections on the nation as a carnal reality', Human Rights Service, 14 December 2009, https://www.rights.no/2009/12/reflections-on-the-nation-as-a-carnal-reality/ (last accessed 30 August 2017).
47. Speech, Paris, 19 November 2011.
48. Seminar on Defence, 3 December 2011.
49. Speech, Paris, 1 May 2011.
50. Ibid.
51. François Hollande was known as 'the normal president' for his seemingly uneventful personal life and calm, statesmanlike demeanour, in contrast with the 'bling-bling presidency' of his predecessor, Nicolas Sarkozy.
52. Speech, La Baule, 26 September 2012.
53. Speech, Paris, 1 May 2016.
54. Speech, Paris, 19 November 2011.
55. Speech, Metz, 12 December 2011.
56. Speech, La Baule, 26 September 2012.
57. Speech, Paris, 19 November 2011.
58. Speech, Bordeaux, 22 January 2012.
59. The expression '*cheval de retour*' is used as a pun, meaning both 'warhorse' and 'recidivist'.
60. Speech, Paris, 1 May 2013.
61. Speech, Metz, 12 December 2011.
62. Speech, Marseille, 6 September 2015.
63. Speech, Paris, 19 November 2011.
64. Speech, Saint-Denis, 9 January 2012.
65. Speech, La Baule, 26 September 2012.
66. Speech, Paris, 10 December 2015.

67. Speech, Lille, 20 March 2014.
68. Speech, Metz, 12 December 2011.
69. Speech, Marseille, 15 September 2013.
70. Speech, Bordeaux, 22 January 2012.
71. Ibid.
72. Speech, Marseille, 4 March 2012.
73. Speech, Bordeaux, 22 January 2012.
74. Speech, Saint-Laurent-du-Var, 7 September 2010.
75. Speech, La Baule, 26 September 2012.
76. Ibid. She referred to the 'survival of France' again in a speech in Paris on 1 May 2013.
77. Speech, Marseille, 6 September 2015.
78. Speech, Châteauroux, 26 February 2012.
79. This mythologization of politics and history is thoroughly analysed in Alduy and Wahnich, *Marine Le Pen prise aux mots*, pp. 179–85.
80. Ibid., p. 124.
81. Speech, Bordeaux, 22 January 2012.
82. Ibid.
83. Speech, Saint-Laurent-du-Var, 7 September 2010.
84. Speech, Metz, 12 December 2011.
85. Speech, Toulouse, 5 February 2012.
86. Speech, Paris, 10 December 2015.
87. Speech, Paris, 1 May 2013.
88. Speech, Paris, 10 December 2015.
89. Speech, Paris, 1 May 2013.
90. Ibid.
91. Speech, Paris, 19 November 2011.
92. See Alduy and Wahnich, *Marine Le Pen prise aux mots*, pp. 145–6.
93. Speech, Bordeaux, 22 January 2012 (emphasis added).

The biblical story of the torn temple veil and the death of Christ has a longstanding place in esoteric thought. It also has obvious contemporary connotations of Islam and one of its features most frequently argued to be incompatible with the Republic's secularism: some Muslim women's wearing of a headscarf or veil in public spaces.

EPILOGUE TO THE ENGLISH EDITION

1. A feminist activist group famous globally for their topless protests in support of women's rights. Though founded in Ukraine, its largest membership is in France.
2. Institut français d'opinion publique, 'Le profil des électeurs et les clefs du premier tour des élections législatives', 11 June 2017, http://www.ifop.com/media/poll/3791-1-study_file.pdf (last accessed 31 August 2017).